To Jim & Micke

from Bill

October 26, 1998

Existentialism

Universal Standard Encyclopedia Vol 8 p. 3012
Standard Reference Works Pub. Co. Inc. N.Y 1956

A literary + philosophical movement which came into existence in France in 1943, under the leadership of Jean Paul Sartre based on the tenets formulated in his philosophical study, L'Être et le Néant (1943)
Sources/E - German philosophy of phenomenology
- certain postulates of Danish philosopher Sören Kierkegaard;
basic theory/E - contained in wds/Descartes, "I think; therefore I am"

Accdg to E. reality is defined by the mind, + has no meaning apart from man's recognition of it.
yet an outer collective reality exists, creating a disparity and contradiction between man's inner self and " " position + function in real world

The basic pattern of existence is therefore senseless,
but
the responsibility for man's life
(because E-ists deny traditional divine guidance)
is in man's hands.

The individual is responsible for every movement he makes + in the end he is the complete result of his own actions

this responsibility, according to E creates innate sense/anguish from which he can hope to emancipate himself only by realizing himself to his fullest extent.

The Ethics of Kant and Brunner

Contemporary Existentialism

Howard Slaatte
General Editor

Vol. 6

PETER LANG
New York • Washington, D.C./Baltimore • Boston
Bern • Frankfurt am Main • Berlin • Vienna • Paris

William H. Bailey

The Ethics of Kant and Brunner

An Existential Blend

PETER LANG
New York • Washington, D.C./Baltimore • Boston
Bern • Frankfurt am Main • Berlin • Vienna • Paris

Library of Congress Cataloging-in-Publication Data

Bailey, William H.
The ethics of Kant and Brunner: an existential blend / William H. Bailey.
p. cm. — (Contemporary existentialism; vol. 6)
Includes bibliographical references (p.) and index.
1. Existential ethics. 2. Kant, Immanuel, 1724–1804—Ethics. 3. Brunner, Emil, 1899–1966—Ethics. 4. Christianity and existentialism. 5. Christian ethics. 6. Law and ethics. 7. Justice (Philosophy). 8. Christianity and justice. I. Title. II. Series.
BJ1340.B35 170'.92'2—dc20 96-33953
ISBN 0-8204-3133-8
ISSN 0895-0520

Die Deutsche Bibliothek-CIP-Einheitsaufnahme

Bailey, William H.:
The ethics of Kant and Brunner: an existential blend / William H. Bailey.
–New York; Washington, D.C./Baltimore; Boston; Bern;
Frankfurt am Main; Berlin; Vienna; Paris: Lang.
(Contemporary existentialism; Vol. 6)
ISBN 0-8204-3133-8
NE: GT

The paper in this book meets the guidelines for permanence and durability of the Committee on Production Guidelines for Book Longevity of the Council of Library Resources.

Printed in the United States of America.

To my wife Grace
without whom I could not have
completed this book.

TABLE OF CONTENTS

PREFACE

One writer notes that Kierkegaard knew he needed an idea to live for, and that Christianity was his "radical cure." So he decided to take the cure. In a real sense this book offers a cure of sorts in the area of Christian living and Christian thought. We start to look at our faith as the beginning of our journey. Before we can really know the meaning of natural law or the real meaning of positive law, we must have ourselves take "the leap of faith." In other words, faith gives meaning, and faith finally has to deal with justice and law.

Although it may sound strange, Moses could be considered an early existentialist. When the Lord calls Moses out of the burning bush, Moses answers, "Here I am." When the Lord told Moses that he was going to send Moses to Egypt to deal with Pharaoh, Moses asks, "When I deal with them and they ask me your name, what shall I tell them?" The Lord told Moses to tell them "I am" (Yahweh) has sent me. So Moses does lead the Hebrews out of Egypt and across the Sea of Reeds. Finally, after much struggle, Moses leads his people to the region of Sinai. The people sometimes listened to Moses and sometimes not. The Lord told Moses to get the people, through careful preparation, ready for a message. On the third day, the Lord spoke to them through smoke, thunder, and lightning, giving them the Ten

Commandments.

The Lord led the Hebrews through the wilderness teaching them to know the Presence. In this real existential experience, Moses talked with God as man to man. The point I am making is that faith had to be the basis of Moses' work and the Lord's gift. So we need an existential view and a sense of presence.

Through the centuries since that time, lawyers and legal thinkers have been impelled to think of a law for all the people. This law, early on, was called the law of nature. With the experience of Yahweh and his possession of the Ten Commandments there was law that came in time to be called natural law. This law was given by God's instilling a special type of law through reason. Natural law went back as far as Aristotle. Laws might be written, but reason was in back of the formation of positive law to give them force and reality.

Natural law was the basic law during the Revolutionary War and continued past Coolidge to fairly modern times. Coolidge said that law was "found" and not just written.

Natural law is the work of reason watched over by the Divine Legislator. Those who held to natural law saw it as giving through God's leading a form of positive law. Natural law began before Aristotle and came in various forms and shapes though surprisingly, even Christian versions have not changed its working as much as we would think.

From the earliest times in this country, natural law was a part of the thinking and working of the legal system. The historical, mechanical, and then sociological law, did a lot to lessen the use of natural law. Finally, it disappeared from the thinking of most jurisprudence. Overall, I suppose we could say that natural law had its last major use by the West in the Nuremberg Trials.

The major thrust of this study is the concern for justice, Kant and Brunner exemplifying this concern. Dr. Howard Slaatte, in a letter to me some time ago, notes that Kant saw the importance of transcendent theology as the "Censor of reason." Reason was the basis of his faith, and he used his reason in such a way.

Paul Tillich feels that in religious thought there has been a renewal of interest in Kant. The Ritschlians felt that Kant had a certainty in his writing. They felt he left but one window out of our finitude, the moral imperative. The real basis for certainty is the moral point of view. Religion is that which makes us able to actualize ourselves. We do this as moral persons. Religion is a supporting power of the ethical.

Brunner seeks to get at justice in his own special way. A highly relevant comment is that justice says we need to give each person his due. This is not the same as saying each person gets exactly the same. Yet justice is related to equality. Brunner's thought is still related to equality. Brunner was also great in his writing on the orders of creation and his thought on natural law.

In this work, we mainly consider two ethical thinkers, Kant and Brunner. We are appreciative of their concern for justice which they say is each man getting his due. Kant talks about the good will which would produce the same effect. There are obviously differences in many places, but they have much in common. Both men are in some measure existential. Kroner talks about Kant's having "an existential flavor." Slaatte and Hopper think of Brunner as being existential, a crisis theologian early in his life and then a neo-orthodox thinker, but always influenced by Kierkegaard's existentialism. Seeing this much we can think about Kant and Brunner in terms of an existential blend.

Kant writes about the church as being an ethical commonwealth, for example, people under ethical laws whose supreme head and lawgiver is God. He is not writing about a theocracy based on a government of priests, but on an institution where laws are primarily inward. Brunner thinks more about the Kingdom of God, where God rules and peace reigns.

The Ethics of Kant and Brunner

Existential Blend

William H. Bailey

CHAPTER I

Historical Introduction

Man always has God or an idol. He can no more rid himself of this dimension of his existence than he can rid himself of the dimensions of time. When man has God, man is doing what the best requires of him. But when man is drawn into the realm of sin, he pushes God away and chooses to go his own way. Man, when he serves God, can expect to get his due. When man is on the right path he sees that this justice when done points to law. In seeking to understand the content of law in earlier people, we find that Aristotle came up with natural law. Natural law was seen as what God willed. This idea passed through many Greek and Latin philosophers. Cicero had a large influence on natural law. He regarded natural law as the basis of law in general. Doubtless, he had a great influence on Christian natural law. The natural law ran its course through the medieval period. People like Fichte and Kant had a large background in natural law. Rousseau and Christian Wolff also did a lot with natural law. In some translations, Kant is translated as using the word "nature" as a synonym of the law of nature.

Natural law continued to have a place in the nineteenth century. In this country, people like Story, Lincoln, and many justices of the courts appealed to natural law.

One thing we need to emphasize is that natural law tried to keep clear the ideas of right and wrong. It has sought to keep both the individual and the government centered. The big consideration is keeping a clear emphasis on moral thought.

As implied earlier, Aristotle passed for centuries as the father of natural law.[1] His knowledge and his formulation of ethics had an important place in his and later thinkers' understanding. His broad understanding made an excellent foundation, for law finds its existence in the will of the lawmaker. That which is right is permanent. Positive law embodies this teaching to an important extent. Natural law, however, goes way beyond the teaching of positive law. Natural law has to be realized in the positive law, since positive law takes the ideas and gives them reality.

In time, Stoicism was founded by a philosopher named Zeno, who lived around 340 to 265 B.C. The Stoics denied the Aristotelian view that happiness was a necessity. They taught that people could be happy without good food and friends. This position was possible for the Stoics, because they believed in extreme rationality and a devaluing of human emotions. They held to a less extreme biological form of naturalism placing human beings in a different form of natural things. The Stoics stressed the difference between customs and laws of society, and the unchanging role of reason was given form in a certain cosmopolitanism. The cosmopolitan gave good place to reason and recognized all human beings as fellow citizens.[2]

The broad conception of a rational law binding different cultures appealed to the Christian world as well. This restrained concern gave them a sense of kinship with the Stoics. Christians appreciated the Stoics' emphasis on reason. The cosmopolitan recognizes all humans as fellow citizens. Christians were also attracted to the Stoics because of their emphasis on human dignity and freedom. St. Thomas Aquinas gave the theory of natural law its classic expression bringing together the Aristotelian, the Stoic, and the Christian elements.

There is much that can be said about politicians who have studied law. George Washington attended William and Mary. In one of his speeches he noted, "Let us with caution indulge the supposition that morality can be maintained without religion. Reason and experience forbid us to expect public morality in the absence of religious principle." Without religious and moral principles, we are unwise to expect family values to be executed. Today young people commit all kinds of violent acts. They carry weapons and are not hesitant about using them. This is in sharp contrast to what occurred in schools during the forties. I heard Billy Graham say on TV that the big misdemeanors in schools of the forties were throwing spitballs, running on the stairs, and whispering in class. What a difference fifty years has made!

John Adams, our second president, believed freedom and democracy were possible when men realized that the Constitution was made for moral and religious purposes. To have a different kind of government is not possible, and if we don't have religious faith, our freedom will be eroded. Washington and Adams believed that without faith in the Bible, governments run amok.

If people don't believe in eternal life, they readily ask what harm there can be in hedonism.[3] Those who misuse the Constitution to exclude religion from the public schools, the public square, and the deliberations of elected bodies are those who are enemies of the Constitution itself.

The base document which is a challenge to our morality and even our faith is the Declaration of Independence, which refers to a Creator who gives us inalienable rights. Jefferson warned the nation that our liberties may be insecure unless we realize that our liberties are "a gift of God." We are told that a Houston man did an analysis of the writings of the founders of our country. He found that 34% of the quotes in these writings were taken directly from the Bible and another 60% was inspired by its teachings.[4] We cannot understand the reason for our forefathers' faith unless we understand their reliance on the Bible.

William and Mary was founded in 1693, the original charter calling for the school to pursue education that serves the cause of Christ, to train pastors, to educate youth piously, and to endeavor to propagate the faith among the western Indians.[5] One hundred twenty-three out of the one hundred twenty-six colleges in early America were founded to further the faith. Woodrow Wilson, noting how so many in the country had lost their faith, wrote that a nation which does not remember what its past was does not know what it is doing today nor what it is trying to do in the future.[6]

In the realm of private law, Americans took over the common law. In the realm of public law, they took over the natural law. Natural law was the background of law in America, particularly in the realm of constitutional law. Common law, as such, was hardened, and only slowly did equity law come to bring relief. The doctrine of natural law, dominant in England and on the Continent in the seventeenth and eighteenth centuries, had played its part.

In time, the historical school of jurisprudence came upon the scene, and then mechanical law came to have a big part in the thinking of some of the Supreme Court justices. Dean Roscoe Pound said that the use of mechanical law, such as stare decisis, was the etiquette of justice. When Pound with his fellow judges, Holmes and Brandeis, saw that historical law was too confining, they revolted from form to function. Law was made for man from concepts to activities, from statistics to dynamics. They sought to make law deal with the present, challenging the jurists who thought of themselves above the battle. Pound was seeing a new kind of law based upon philosophy and the social sciences. He called this sociological jurisprudence, a movement toward pragmatism and a new way of thinking about law. The engineer is judged by what he does and whether his work is adequate. Sociological jurisprudence was a shift from the abstract to the relative, from doctrines to practices, from passive (and therefore pessimistic) determinism, to creative action, and therefore to freedom. Sociological law would be concerned with collective social good. Benefits of this thinking were found in constitutional law and public policy.[7]

Before moving to historical jurisprudence, it should be said that believers in natural law felt that natural law was not just written, it was discovered. Coolidge once said that it was also a gift to have natural law be the director of our positive law.

"Historical jurisprudence was evolution applied to law. It was not an evolution which afforded grounds for progress or left room for reform. It was rather like the Spencerean evolution which condemned human institutions to the slow processes of history and tradition."[8] This process was slow and reactionary and only gradually penetrated natural law. It was a merging with natural law rather than supplanting it. Law thus became more scholarly but less philosophical.

Men like Field and Brewer believed in the rules of mechanical law, thus interpreting the Constitution rather as a prohibition than an instrument. This sort of thinking influenced courts from the 1880s to the 1930s. During this time the field was covered with the corpses of social welfare laws, natural law and historical jurisprudence having a strong hold on lawyers' and judges' minds.[9]

We have been, as it were, on a tour through the law. The natural law of early days was the director of our choice, and our guide. The feeling existed that God had made the law and that he still worked to give law scope. Law seemed to be governed by the historical material. Then the mechanical emphasis took over, seeking to place fine restrictions on the law. Law was laid along side of the Constitution, and if the law fit mechanically, then the law was acceptable. In reaction to this trend came the liberalism of the Warren Court, in which the judiciary became almost legislative.

Particularly affected by this trend have been religious rights which have become an important part of our national life. Many appeals have been made to the First Amendment. These problems have often been concerned with schools. The Mergens case was one of these. A young woman started a Bible club in school, but the school ruled that this was not permissible. Bridget and her father sued and the case eventually wound up in the Supreme Court. The case entered the law books as West Side Community Schools v. Mergens. The Court rules that as long as the students were in charge of the meetings, the club was constitutional.

Another important case was Lamb's Chapel v. Center Morishes Union Free School. This case involved a church that asked permission to use the school for the showing of the James Dobson film, *Turn Your Hearts toward Home*. The school felt that the film was religious, and therefore denied the request even though other community groups were allowed to use the school. The case went through all the lower courts, and finally ended up in the Supreme Court. Jay Sekulow, chief attorney for the American Center for Law and Justice, argued the case for the church, citing unfairness on the part of the school since other groups used the school and the film was a family film. The school apparently felt that church activities should be within the four walls of the church. Sekulow argued that this was censorship. Free speech is free when it is open and allowed. He apparently convinced the justices that this was a case in violation of the First Amendment. The justices ruled unanimously for Lamb's Chapel.[10]

Prayer in public school had generally been allowed. Daniel Weisman sued when his daughter didn't want to attend a graduation at which prayer was offered. When the case finally reached the Supreme Court, many felt that school prayer would be retained. However, Justice Kennedy is said to have changed his mind and was chosen to write for the majority. Their decision was that ministers, priests, and rabbis could no longer have prayer at graduations. They were seen as part of official administration, and this could be interpreted as governmental approval of a particular religion.

Another similar case soon came to court, Jones v. Clear Creek. The Fifth Federal District tried the case. Their determination was that though ministers cannot offer prayer at graduations, senior students could. This case went to the Supreme Court, but the Court sent it back to the Fifth Federal District, which meant ultimately that students could offer prayer at graduations but school or ministerial officials could not.

In the "See You at the Pole" case, a group of students in Texas gathered around their school's flagpole to pray. The school opposed this but was informed by Sekulow that student-initiated prayer was legal. This movement soon spread to other schools. It is interesting to note that when schools in this country were opposing "See You at the Pole," Russian students prayed in Red Square and at Lenin's tomb.[11]

Endnotes

1. Aristotle has generally been thought of as the father of natural law. However he himself seems to have felt that natural law was as old as philosophy. Just as wonder, according to Aristotle, lies at the beginning of philosophy so too it is found at the beginning of natural law. Heinrich A. Rommen, *The Natural Law,* trans. by Thomas B. Hanley, p. 103.
2. Michael D. Boyles and Kenneth Henley, editors, *Right Conduct,* pp. 14, 15.
3. Hedonism as here used may seem too strong a word, but hedonism means a seeking of unguided pleasure. Certainly this is what we observe when God is removed from the public square.
4. Ibid.
5. Ibid.
6. Ibid.
7. Henry Steele Commager, *The American Mind*, p. 336-337.
8. Ibid.
9. Ibid.
10. Jay Sekulow, *Law and Justice*, p. 3.
11. Nancy Gibbs, *Time*, December 9, 1991, pp. 60-66.

CHAPTER II

To Will One Thing

In his struggle about the time of his conversion Kierkegaard suggested that he needed Christ to come to him through closed doors. A month later he writes about the "indescribable joy" which seized him in 1838. In other words, he experienced conversion and another month later he was at confession and Holy Communion. As a result of his conversion he became reconciled with his father. It also influenced him to attend the pastoral seminarium. However, Kierkegaard was never ordained.

Kierkegaard became engaged to Regina Olson, but the engagement didn't last long. He felt he did not have the ability to live with it. However, the experience seemed to set a flame of genius alight in Kierkegaard. He always regarded the engagement as a religious experience in itself, one which set him on the path of writing. Most of us would not want the experience of a broken engagement but Kierkegaard felt his faith was deepened. The price he paid was a benefit to all of us religiously.[1]

In 1848, Kierkegaard had a further decisive experience which deepened his resolve to "will one thing." On Wednesday, April 19, he said, "My whole being is changed," his self-isolation broken. In spite of his deepening faith he came to believe that the Danish church was weak and emaciated. However, he felt that the church, though weak, had some strengths and affirmed the Chalcedonian Creed.

By his leap from nothingness to faith Kierkegaard enabled us to see the power of this faith. Some cynics see it as a leap out of nothingness into faith and then into nothingness again.

Kierkegaard helps us with committed reason to find our true selves. Unamuno sees this as a push for understanding and comments, "My mission is to seek the truth in life and life in truth. My mission is to struggle tirelessly and without ceasing to deal with the unknown."[2] He says this is a mission to struggle with God as Jacob did with the angel at Jabock from dark until dawn. This would indicate that God is intensely personal, not obscured by objective ideas of human reason.[3]

Yet man, made in the image of God, is a being of spirit and flesh. This duality means that if there were no intellectual tension with man there would be no crisis for man. The Christian existentialist tries to uphold tension in terms of Christian existence. This helps to get Christian theology off the ground in a secular age. Theology does offer a language in which such meaning can be expressed. The interpretation of theology within terms of contemporary philosophy is justified. The Biblical view sees man standing out from the inanimate and animate world. The Bible sees polarities in man symbolized by the dust of the ground and the breath of life, or flesh and spirit. So the existentialist is aware of the tension between man's freedom and his finitude, his possibilities and his guilt. Just as the Bible speaks of faith so the existentialist sees the need for man to take up attitudes in the world without knowing the possibilities. More than this the existentialist agrees with the Bible in stressing priorities and the distinctiveness of the personal. The existentialist seeks to get man to consider the future which persuades him to talk about God. It helps to link theology with proclamation to show the relevance of the preacher, as he seeks to conform the life of the church to the demands of the Gospel, for a philosophy that arises from the concrete experience of existence back to a world of deep understanding. In insisting that dogmas have to do with man and his life with God, we use the existential approach to prevent theology from straying into an abstract scholasticism, and keep it near the life of the church.[4]

Kierkegaard had a little different approach at this point. For him freedom was the center of thought. The single individual must have first priority. Kierkegaard talks about a secret inwardness. To love God and your fellow man is like opening two doors at the same time. It is impossible to have one shut and the other open. At times, Kierkegaard talks about the collision of the opposites, yet at other times his writings reflect the saying that defining existentialism is like trying to define a flavor or an odor.

Probably, we can say in our search that "Existentialism is a way of life which involves one's self." Kierkegaard could be that serious yet on another occasion he wrote, "From the Christian view point faith belongs to the existentialist." God did not appear in the character of a professor who has some doctrines which must be believed and then understood.[5] Some existentialists write in poetry, drama, or whatever, but Kierkegaard wrote in what he called "indirect communication," his way of saying that his writing was not just to inform. He wanted his readers to "exist," wanted them to be individuals. He wanted his readers, in most cases professors, preachers, and students to "live" life and not be bound to those who would have preferred the propositional and abstract to the personal and active. Kierkegaard preferred the poetic at times, and at other times "the unscientific."

Existentialism involves more of what you do than what you think. Definitions of thought would betray by thinking propositions when action is needed. This is why academic philosophers cannot accept existentialism.

In the matter of understanding existentialism, Ortega y Gasset has been a little tough on Heidegger when it comes to understanding what Heidegger says. The trouble is that the same antidote covers a lot of other existentialists as well. Gasset says that Heidegger in his use of words reminds him of a diver diving for pearls. He goes deep down to bring up hidden pearls between his teeth, but it may be questioned whether Heidegger ever comes back up. Some thinkers feel that the search is deep and not too clear. We must keep our ears to the ground if we are going to learn and do existentially. It sounds easy, but really learning what existentialism is all about is not that easy.

We usually think of Kierkegaard as being the first existentialist, but Socrates certainly did his bit to make people really come to grips with existential living. His questions made the wisest humble. Others might think of St. Paul as an early existentialist for whom intellectual doubt carried with it a threat of meaninglessness. He saw guilt and death as the realities that measured man.[6]

Existentialism is always concerned with truth. Most truths are not truths until they are related to an existing individual. Josiah Royce tells about the little boy who would not replace his broken lead soldier for another even though it was cast from the same mold. Was the boy stubborn? Not at all! He was just a junior existentialist. The individual was more important than the universal. This is not the Kantian model which sees in every man the essence of mankind in general and from that inferred the rights of all individuals the same. It is rather the nineteenth-century individualism of Goethe and Nietzsche who saw in each man a singular life, unrepeatable in anyone else, untransferable to anyone else. We infer from this that the rights of each man are unique. It was to this individualism to which Heidegger and Jaspers appealed when they realized that no man can die another man's death for him. There are no general molds in which all men are cast. Doing is the principle many people gather from existentialism, yet we cannot infer that there is no social life in existentialism. It is only true that social relations are not based upon an abstract eighteenth-century view of the individual.

To exist means to reach beyond one's own being. To exist means to stand outside one's self, to extend beyond one's self. When a seriously existing man allows his life to undergo interrogation to its roots he will sense his life as bottomless. The danger seen in the existential individual, therefore, is that one will remain locked up in isolation from society, a heart curved in upon itself. Man's dominant passions are social and centrifugal, the passion of the inner man urging him to move beyond himself to an alliance providing stability. Man has to be careful not to reach out to the inauthentic object. This can be viewed as idolatry.

The biggest gap between current philosophies and existentialism is that existentialism does not want to be bound by the sciences. Kierkegaard repudiated the scientific in Hegel's system.[7]

What is the connection between existentialism and biography? Writers on existentialism spend a lot of time on a few philosophers, largely Kierkegaard. Such knowledge can be helpful. We would have to say that each life is unique. As someone has written, we can never learn to exist merely by imitating Kierkegaard. That person will only end by breaking up his chief romance, being ashamed of his father, and dying at forty-two. One must learn to participate in the spirit and thought life that Kierkegaard showed. Doubtless it would be better to face our own romance, care for and understand our father, share our guilt and concern about death. When we read existentialist biography, we should read it with the intent of improving our own lives. Kierkegaard suggested that biography should assume the properties of a nettle. When you touch it you become more aware of yourself than the nettle.

Many of the existentialists have written their biographies in one form or another. Taking them for what they are we should not be disappointed. Such biographical material should not be for gossip, for instance; think what gossip could do with, "The Diary of a Seducer." These biographies should give us understanding about our own lives.[8] Of course, we emphasize the concrete existence not abstract concepts.

What about the interrelatedness between existentialism and Christianity? We know that existentialists range from Kierkegaard to Nietzsche, from Sartre to Marcel. Of course, there are many others, some going one way and some another. What about existentialism and Christianity? There are people in the Bible who certainly exhibit existential tendencies of a sort. Moses had such an experience when he found out the name of Yahweh and when he confronted and talked to God in the wilderness. The cloud by day and the pillar of fire by night indicate some really deep experience. I don't know how we can keep from seeing these as existential experiences. They were not ivory tower dreams or theories.

Isaiah in the temple receiving his call from God and sent out to carry the faith is another of the Old Testament worthies. Jeremiah's call and his answer are other examples. To the Lord's call, Jeremiah answers, "Ah, Lord Yahweh, I cannot go for I am only a boy." Another of these experiences is Solomon dedicating the temple. The choir is singing and the presence of Yahweh is so great the choir members have to leave the temple. Of course, Paul has many experiences, but the road to Damascus meeting with the living Jesus is a great one.

Some of the great mystics are seen as existential mystics, but this is perhaps reading too much into them. However, the mystics do have some important things to say. Apparently, Karl Barth became indifferent to existentialism after his early experience with Kierkegaard. Barth writes, "In all the theological-philosophical soup today there floats some philosophical fragments."[9] Michalson says that Nietzsche became violent over his feeling that the German Protestant pastor is the father of German philosophy.[10] Whatever the case, existentialism is now a telling influence. Carl Michalson refers to existentialism as a road to Bethlehem, or better, Calvary.[11]

It could be said that Kierkegaard is a Christian Socrates. Kierkegaard's reflection leads less to the individual's discovery of his ignorance than of guilt and the utter contingency of being. Man exists less in knowledge and more in faith. His ruler is Jesus Christ; the comic and the tragic in life appear in Christian perspective as the comic disproportion between the disciple and the Master he undertakes to imitate, and so his tragic participation is the cross.

As Kierkegaard struggled with life about him, he had a sharp eye, one of the sharpest, for duplicity. He saw the comedy and tragedy in preaching. He demonstrated the meekness of Jesus Christ and sought confidently to help us understand the might of Christianity. He thought it was tragic when preachers with great solemnity read for the congregation of well-dressed, well-fed, well-taught solid leading citizens the text from the apostle Paul, "Consider your call, brethran, not many were wise according to worldly standards, not many were powerful, not many of noble birth, but God chose what is foolish in the world to shame the wise, God chose what is low and despised in the world, even things that are not to bring to nothing the things that are."[12]

Before a Christian who is trying to become a true Christian there stands the hiddenness of God. God is utterly different from himself, different in his eternity and different in his holiness. There is a strangeness here, the strangeness of God who becomes a man, of the man who is God. We note that Kierkegaard is a Chalcedonian Christian who maintains that what we have before us as believers is a doctrine about the dogma of the incarnation.

We recognize that Kierkegaard was a church reformer, insisting that what the state and sects needed to do was to become a witness to the truth, to direct man away from himself to the eternal, to Christ, to the Ultimate, the Absolute.

True Christianity as it exists in living subjects or as living selves who become themselves by becoming true Christians, are a becoming, not a being. It is becoming eternal, true, a being with only one aim, and that an absolute one. Becoming a Christian is not a painless process of growth. It is a becoming by the self by faith what it is not possible for the self to become by itself. We say it is becoming what God wants us to become. It is a becoming of free men who must free themselves. St. Paul says, "Work out your own salvation for it is God working in you."[13]

We can summarize what existentialism is saying to us simply. The most impressive existentialist Kierkegaard stresses the importance of practical firsthand decisions and involvement as over against intellectual involvement as mere assent to an abstract truth. Kierkegaard strongly attacked the nominally orthodox man who was not normally committed. It is personal commitment rather than abstract reason which brings a person into relationship with God.[14] "Faith," he said, is "an absolute relation to the Absolute. It is total self-commitment."

We might mention that there are atheistic existentialists like Sartre. There are also philosophers like the Catholic thinker, Gabriel Marcel, who even though he was a friend of Sartre, did not agree with Sartre's brand of existentialism.

This simple summary of existentialism can obscure the need to understand the problem. Until Mt. Sinai, Moses was in effect law along with those whom he appointed to help rule. The Lord decided to give the Ten Commandments as law from Mt. Sinai. The existentialism of Presence was real in God's voice and command. On the third day, the Lord sent smoke, thunder, and lightning. The Lord had Moses and Aaron climb the mountain with him and when he spoke the people all trembled. This was the beginning of a series of laws which has stood by itself, but also served as a model for much of our law since that time.

We can say that Moses emphasized the vitality of faith, in a way that is existential. In Deuteronomy 5, Moses tells the people that God made a covenant with them, not their fathers. "The Lord spoke to you face to face out of fire on the mountain."

The Lord had told them, "You shall have no other gods nor worship them. You shall not make graven images [the way their neighbors did]." And so the commands went until there were ten. Certainly, there were laws before the Ten Commandments such as Hammurabi's laws. The Ten Commandments, however, were to be the model for the Christian world. We are going to be talking later on about natural law, and some will wonder what the relationship is between natural law and the Ten Commandments. The commandments and other laws in the Bible will be the basis of the requirements of God as far as they go. However, there is more that the rational and Christian man needs to know about law and justice. God has created the world, and he put reason into the nature of the universe" manufacturer's directions." Justice looks to the law above the law. The model, also, becomes the standard for legislation. This is the model that lawmakers take into consideration when they seek to abolish unjust laws and create just laws. When a man protests against injustice, he does so in the spirit of this law, which becomes a guide for the blind, a light for those who are in darkness which Paul says in Romans 2:19, the unwritten law as Paul says in Romans 11. This unwritten law is written into the hearts of men and should work to create permanence in all human thought about the law and all human systems.[15]

Endnotes

1. T. H. Croxall, *Glimpses and Impressions of Kierkegaard*, p. xv.
2. Howard Slaatte, *The Paradox of Existentialist Theology*, quotes Miguel Unamuno, p. 167.
3. Carl Michalson, ed., *Christianity and the Existentialists*, 1956, p. 10.
4. Tim Dowley, ed., *Eerdmans' Handbook to the History of Christianity*, p. 139.
5. Ibid.
6. Carl Michalson, ed., *Christianity and the Existentialists*, p. 9.
7. Carl Michalson, ed., *Christianity and the Existentialists*, Michalson's article, "What is Existentialism," p. 16.
8. Ibid., p. 19.
9. *Theological Studies*, Heft 34 1952, quoted by Michalson, in "What is Existentialism," p. 20, *Christianity and the Existentialists*.
10. Ibid.
11. Ibid.
12. Carl Michalson, ed., *Christianity and the Existentialists*, Richard Niebuhr, "Soren Kierkegaard," p. 35.
13. Ibid., p. 40.
14. *Eerdman's Handbook to the History of Christianity*, p. 600.
15. Romans 7:6.

CHAPTER III

Where Can We Find Justice

We have to Search

The meaning of justice is one of the pressing problems of our time. The unsettled condition in our own country as to a Christian understanding of justice points at the need to try to find out. There is no one controlling and unifying philosophy for our civilization as there was, for example, in the medieval period. Perhaps, the sociological thinkers on legal philosophy have had the greatest influence on modern positive law. This philosophy is inadequate in its lack of a transcendent perspective, as well as in an understanding of the nature of man. Positivism in legal thought is even more glaringly inadequate in both doctrines. It applies in a too thoroughgoing fashion the criteria and laws of the physical sciences to man. The physical laws of the universe apply to man, but man is more than the elements of even the animal level.

The import of this work is that Christian norms are the only answer, more particularly, the norms of Protestant Christianity point out the solution to man's legal problems. Roman Catholics for many centuries have thought upon the problems of justice and legal philosophy. Protestants have not done as much work in this area. This is surprising in view of the strong desire and the real search for ways to establish the Christian commonwealth. Even where there was a search for a separate holy community of saints, as in the Plymouth Settlement in New England, the emphasis was upon practice as the Bible commanded, rather than new thought on justice as it related to law. The Bible was determinative for the saints in their church and personal devotions. The common law of England was a part of the Pilgrim's heritage and, as such, was not repudiated when it came to doing business in the workaday world. The Jamestown settlement in Virginia had been required to "adhere" as closely as it could "to the common law and the equity thereof."[1]

There was no lawyer in the original Plymouth settlement, however, as soon as lawyers came to the settlement the common law was in use. Undoubtedly, before that time as much of the law as was known by the laymen of the colony was applied. Certainly, very early there was legal talent in Massachusetts Bay.[2] Governor Winthrop was trained in the Courts of Lincoln Inn in London and had held important positions in England before migrating to New England.[3]

The stern Biblical Calvinism of the Puritans had steeled them to the belief that every man had to live by his own choices, hence there was a predilection for the common law, as over against equity. This stern adherence to decisions once made was carried through into modern times and tended to align Protestants with laissez-faire capitalism in too many cases. The reasoning back of this adherence to laissez-faire capitalism was that each man was free to make his own contract in capitalism, and he ought to be let alone to carry out his bargain. If he broke his contract, there was always proper legal remedy. In the case of the employee, there was always the remedy of dismissal.[4]

This tendency to laissez-faire capitalism aligned with the eighteenth-century concept of natural law and mechanical jurisprudence made for a hardening of the law to a point where all change was frowned upon.[5] Along with mechanical jurisprudence, there was added the Blackstonean emphasis on the mystery of the law to protect ultimate values.[6] This combination of emphases brought about a situation wherein law was applied in a certain way just because it had always been done that way. "It is revolting," Holmes wrote as early as

1897, "to have no better reason for a rule of law than that it was laid down in the time of Henry IV."[7] Commager caustically asserted that it was not revolting at all to many American judges trained in what he termed "black letter law," rather it would be more true to say that they found it imminently right and proper that this be done.[8]

The United States got its private law when the settlers migrated to this country. All the states chose the common law except Louisiana which was secured from France and, therefore, has kept the civil law except for the law of torts.[9]

In the latter half of the nineteenth and the early first part of this century public law relied heavily on natural law theories. When jurists sought to interpret the Constitution, they went back of the Constitution and interpreted the natural law theories which were supposed to be the principles that had made the Constitution. The interpretation they made was quite narrow.

On top of this the common law was interpreted in terms of strict precedents rather than in terms of progressive legal reasoning. Unfortunately, the law of equity was in just about the same position with its set forms and its proper procedure of remedying the inadequacies of the common law. In any case, the same judge in most states sat for both types of cases. He only went through the formality of changing robes. Of course, there were different rules, but these had become just about as set as the common law and were strictly enforced.[10]

The natural law theory was carried on into our time with the presuppositions and prejudices of the earlier time. So Justice McReynolds could assert in the mid-1930s that the exercise of sovereign power by the government over money and currency was a violation of natural law.[11]

Justice Roberts was an adherent of the mechanical theory of jurisprudence. He alleged that all a court does when it nullifies an act of Congress is "to lay the Articles of the Constitution which are involved beside the statue which is challenged and to decide whether the latter squares with the former."[12]

Laws are discovered and not made is the view of the Blackstonean theorist of natural law. They are supposed to be deduced from the nature of the universe. The needs of men are not the primary concern, or at least not the starting point.[13]

Men like Joseph Story knew that there were "eternal principles of right and justice" which ought to control legislation. The next stage was not so fortunate. The group of men in this school were known as the historical school because of their concern with history and custom. They lost themselves in the abstractions of custom and history. Laws under the influence of these men became more scholarly and less philosophical, more specialized but less humane. Lawyers took over the law increasingly as their private domain. Law became remote from reality; it lived upon itself and its past.[14]

Under the influence of the mechanical interpretation of law judges invalidated hundreds of state laws either on the theory that they deprived someone of property or the right to freely contract or on the theory that these statutes did not fit in with their theories of due process of law. The judges assumed that the solution was clear and axiomatic and that they were the only persons who could determine the law. Whenever laws ran afoul of their preconceptions, the law had to give way to their assumptions.[15]

The length the judges went in invalidating laws is unbelievable. An Illinois statute was struck down which sought to limit the hours of women in sweatshops on the grounds that women had liberty of contract just as men did. A law was declared illegal in New York because it was "discriminative against female citizens in denying them equal rights with men in the same pursuit." It was further declared "an arbitrary interference with the right of adult females from working at any time of the day that suited her."[16]

Holmes pointed to the change in his *The Common Law*. Brandeis made this change more explicit in his argument before the Supreme Court in 1908 in Muller v. Oregon in which he used sociological data in such a way that the justices on the bench could not dismiss the cogency of his arguments. This was the first case in which such data had been so used and victory achieved.[17]

Dean Pound furnished much of the philosophical insight for the new approach. He wrote,

> The sociological movement in jurisprudence is a movement for pragmatism as a philosophy of law; for the adjustment of principles and doctrines to the human conditions they are to govern rather than to assume first principles for the human factors in the central place and relegating logic to its true position as an instrument.[18]

The new movement was a reaction against Newtonian concepts applied to the science of law.[19] Law was to be a process, an activity rather than a body of knowledge.

> It is a doing of things, not a serving as passive instruments through which mathematical formulas and mechanical laws realize themselves in the eternally appointed way. The engineer is judged by what he does. His work is judged by its adequacy to the purposes for which it is done, not by its conformity to some ideal of traditional plan.[20]

He wrote in another place, "Where the last century studied only the making of law, they [the sociological thinkers on law] hold it necessary to study as well the means of making legal rules effective."[21] This sociological emphasis is especially interesting when it is remembered that Pound holds a Ph.D. degree in biology along with his degrees in law.

Although Justices Holmes, Brandeis, Cardoza, and Pound brought about a clearer understanding of the social purpose of law, none of them worked out a philosophy of justice that is satisfactory from the Christian point of view.[22] They were more tied to social philosophers than the Christian faith.

The Problem

Both Kant and Brunner see the problem of justice and law as the problem of man. Kant believed that a state of the worst men could be governed well, provided the constitution was a good one. Men may give themselves to the "evil principle," but the will is capable of overcoming the empirical self and of establishing the rule of the noumenal self. The will can will the universal. The state has to use compulsion to guarantee the freedom of each man to do as he wills so long as it does not infringe the equal liberty of others. Kant is essentially and proudly Pelagian. He believed that if a man ought he can.

He appealed to natural law as the basis of rights, but his conception of the natural law is different from that of the "Eighteenth-Century Law of Nature School."[23] His conception is that of the moral law which the reason knows and man can stand in awe of.

Brunner sees the problem of justice and law as the Christian conception of man. The nature of man is such that he has to live according to God's order of creation. When he forgets this order, he loses his rights and comes under the rule of his own tyranny and under the tyranny of the state. The dictatorships of modern times came after men forgot the Fall and came to believe that only the maldistribution of property was the cause of their evil condition and suffering. Autonomous man forgot the source of his right as being in God and his created order. The problem of justice is then the problem of man and his obedience to the law of creation.

It can be readily seen that Kant and Brunner deal differently with the problem raised in the above paragraphs. It will be necessary to see how they deal with some of the principles that relate to the problem of justice. The problem of justice is the problem of man and his place in God's order.

Natural Law

Kant

Kant's theory of natural law did away with the immutable law of the eighteenth century. His theory has to be understood in terms of his concept of the legislative power of the will to will universal law. His concept of the freedom of the will to legislate universals and his concept of the treating of each person as an end, never as a means, was taken by Savigny, a Prussian of Huguenot origin, and others to mean the maximum of liberty to the individual as long as this freedom was not used as a means of harming another person.[24] Herbert Spencer took this over and it became, "Every man is free to do that which he will provided he infringes not the equal liberty of others."[25]

As a legal force, the Kantian idea reached its height of acceptance in Lochner v. New York. In this case, the Supreme Court of the United States invalidated a statute establishing hours of labor for bakers. Justice Holmes dissented in perhaps the most famous dissent in the history of the Supreme Court. He quoted Spencer's injunction and remarked that the citizen's liberty was interfered with by school laws, by the post office, by every state or municipality which takes his money for purposes thought undesirable, whether he likes it or not, and denounced the rules as a "shibboleth." He added the now famous comment, "The Fourteenth Amendment does not enact Mr. Herbert Spencer's 'Social Statistics'."[26]

It seems safe to say that Kant had no thought of applying his maxim in such a manner. Kant seems to have accepted the status quo in economic matters. But his concern for persons would seem to preclude such an approval. He wrote, "Act as if the maxim of your action were to become a universal law."[27] The state enforces by compulsion on the external action of man, but the principle of treating persons as ends and never as means still would apply. However, it would apply only so far as the law of the state was written to enforce it.[28] Ethics makes the principle the core of a man's conduct, while law deals only with the external actions. In ethics, the individual sits as a court upon himself; whereas in the state, law is compulsion by the state toward the desired end. Both are based on his theory of duties.[29]

In spite of the element of compulsion in law, Kant is somewhat individualistic in his philosophy of law. Law is based in the final analysis on the categorical imperative, which is an a priori datum involved in the law of thought. He believed in an a priori existence of the idea of the civil state, which is as early as the state of nature itself. It is true that the state logically came after the social contract, but Kant is not to be put into the category of those who hold to an historical contract. The contract is only an idea of reason, not an historical fact. The contract in not chronologically antecedent, but the logical presupposition of the state.[30]

In the social contract man gives up his freedom to gain it again undiminished, except that wildness is given up to lawful dependence on a law that has sprung from man's own legislative will.[31]

Brunner

Brunner saw that the theory of natural law raises many problems, but he felt that they can be resolved and that natural law serves so great a purpose that the idea cannot be thrown out. Furthermore, the idea corresponds to the truth in the order of God's creation. Thus Brunner's grounding of the natural law is different from Kant's. According to Kant, the pure reason acting in a practical capacity gives the form for the ideal of law. Brunner criticized this as being too abstract and too stoical. He saw the law of nature as an order of creation. This order is created and established by God. It is no abstract formulation of reason but the law of God which men violate to their condemnation and enslavement. There has to be the absolute of justice, otherwise, it is impossible to seriously criticize the godless state when it acts demonically. One can only say, "It does not suit," but there is no further appeal to anything higher.[32]

The law reflects something of the idea of God's creation and his redemption. This is different from an immanent reason which is self-legislative. Brunner questioned whether it is possible to deduce any sort of ethic from the possibility that it may be universal.[33]

ETHICS

Kant

Kant is interested in contracting a pure, moral philosophy cleared of everything empirical. Such a philosophy is possible on the basis of the common ideal of duty and moral law. The moral laws have their relevancy through the ability of the will to will the universal. The will is the one sure good. The good will makes intelligence, judgment, wit, talent, and possession good by the act of willing according to universal laws.[34]

According to Kant, a will is not judged by what it performs, nor by the aptness of the end in view, but is good by the very act of volition. A will is good in itself. If it accomplishes nothing but still wills the good, it is good anyway. Reason establishes a good will as its highest practical distinction. Any end set up must meet the rational requirement.[35]

The end of life cannot be happiness; for men who seek happiness find that it is never attained. Reason gives as its aim not to produce a happy man but to produce an absolutely good will. The will is not complete good, but it is the highest good, and it is the condition of there being a complete good.[36]

If one would know what Kant meant by his concept of the good will, one must start with his thought on duty. Duty is a demand of the will and a good will comes from the heart. It excludes all inclination or desire. Only when a man does his duty because it is required by duty itself can the act be said to have moral value.[37]

Duty is the obligation to act from respect for the moral law. Moral good consists solely in the consciousness of the law itself as determined by the will. Only a rational being can have this consciousness and only he can act to do good without consideration of the consequences of the act.[38]

The will must be clear of every impulse to act for any purpose than duty for duty's sake. Then the next general step is that of conforming the will's action to law. Kant wrote, "Only this conformity to law is to serve the will as principle, that is, I am never to act in any way other than so I could want my maxim also to become general law."[39]

It is necessary to realize that the sole basis of duty is practical reason, which tells us what ought to be done without the least regard to what has been done. This reason arrives at its principles a priori.

Reason must set up its principles of morality entirely independent of experience. Reason deduces acts from laws. The will is the practical expressed in action. Man does not always do what he should. His will recognizes that he ought to obey the moral law willed by the practical reason. Reason commands,

> An objective principle, in so far as it is compulsory for a will and is called a command of reason and the formulation of such a command is called an imperative. Imperatives are expressed by the word ought (or shall) and are indicating thereby the relation of an objective law of reason to will.[40]

The categorical imperative is that which expresses an action as necessary of itself without reference to another end. This imperative is not the imperative of prudence. The hypothetical imperative is not commanded of itself but for another purpose.[41] We can tell nothing about an hypothetical imperative until we know the condition under which it applies, but a categorical imperative can tell at once what it must imply. We are to will in such a way that what we will may become universal law.[42] This leads Kant to his thought of "the Kingdom of ends." The law of rational beings is to treat every person as an end and never as a means. Man is a servant in the kingdom of ends, because he must submit to the universal laws binding upon all. Man is a sovereign because he imposes the law upon himself.

There is one other aspect of Kant's thought that can only be mentioned here. Of freedom Kant wrote:

> Freedom signifies only something that remains when I have eliminated everything belonging to the world of sense from the actuating principles of my will, serving merely the principles of such motives as are taken from the field of sensibility by fixing its limits and showing that it does not contain everything but that there is more beyond it.[43]

Freedom must consist in a will which is a law to itself.

Brunner

According to Brunner, a philosophical ethic can never be combined with the recognition of a divine self-revelation. The use of reason in Kant's ethics presupposes a point of identity between the divine and the human. Transcendental religion can never go along with this teaching. Only God can legislate in the final analysis.[44]

If we try to remove the antithesis between that which is and that which ought to be, we have to split the self into an intelligible self and an empirical self. The intelligible self takes on the legislative function of will and achieving the good. The empirical self becomes sense-bound without freedom. The intelligible self becomes God in man, the Self within the self.[45]

The Kantian ethic bogs down in the simple question: What ought I to do? One cannot help admiring the fact that Kant does not fall a prey to laying down rules and regulations. At the same time, the charge of abstractness has to be made due to the difficulty of getting from the abstract to the concrete.[46]

According to Brunner, Kant knew that there was no union between the world of being and what ought to be except through the symbolism of art or faith in the Creator. He could not choose faith in the Creator, for the reason it would destroy his theory of the autonomy of the will. Kant had to come to terms with eudamonism so that he reached a material ethic after all.[47] He had to recognize natural and material goods without being able from the point of view of his system to evaluate them. He should have become an ascetic in his ethical thought.[48]

From the Christian viewpoint, Brunner thought, man does not owe God anything but love. This love is based on holy fear. Since this is so, the Christian is free to recognize that the Good is that which God does. Man's good then is letting himself be placed within the activity of God.[49]

The problem of the individual and the universal is resolved in confrontation. The command is universal because love is universal. Yet, the command is particular because it is the individual who obeys and who loves in obedience.[50] The antithesis between happiness and duty is done away with. The God who commands and claims man for himself is also the one who gives him life. This is the new law of the spirit.[51]

In Kant's thought, the individual does not need grace. The Christian position, according to Brunner, holds that man cannot enter into God's presence with any merit for the reason that he has none to bring.

There is always the temptation to assert the independence of reason. Reason thinks it can will its own good, therefore, there is no need to seek God's bidding. However, when the Christian comes to know

God, he sees himself absolutely dependent on God. Faith consists in the fact that after the encounter man knows that his life is a gift from God. No longer is there the striving after God.[52]

God takes hold of many by winning our heart, but this atonement has to take place by man's faith. This faith consists in the fact that man knows that life is a gift from God, not a life which is straining after God.

We don't have to take hold of God, God takes hold of us. Brunner wrote:

> The complete reversal of the direction of man's life, constitutes the New Birth, the Divine establishment of the "new man." But the fact that this new birth takes place as conversion, as self-knowledge and the redirection of the Self, is the Divine hallmark of this event, which distinguishes it from a magical process. This is what faith means: to know that one is thus "born again" to accept life as a gift and righteousness as something outside oneself.[53]

The experience of belonging to God brings about something that can never take place in any law. Only love can reveal its meaning. Love is the fulfillment of the law, but it is also the end of natural ethics. That which one ought to do in the spirit of love needs to be done.[54]

Human Nature

Kant

John Smith in a lecture at Yale University honoring Kant's 150th anniversary spoke of a "cosmological" time and defined it as the age "in which man feels sufficiently sure of himself and of his standing in the world to risk a self-forgetful attitude." Man devotes all of his time to control the world around him.[55] Kant was not such a man, although he was greatly interested in the world around him. He was primarily interested in man the subject. If Kant had had a cosmological interest, he would never have wrought a "Copernican revolution" in thought. In this attempt, he set forth to focus attention upon the activity of the rational subject and its relation to the knowing, feeling, or acting self and the type of experience appropriate to these faculties.[56]

Kant believed strongly in man's ability of self-determination through the use of his rational powers. We ought to conform to our morally legislative reason: consequently, we must be able to do so.[57]

He says in another place, "The primary characteristic of the human species is the power as rational beings to acquire a character as such."[58] By character, he means that peculiar "property of the will according to which the subject binds himself to define practical principles which he unalterably prescribed through his reason."[59] He believed in reason as the thing that made man really *man*. It was the legislative power of the will that gave man his moral worth. Kant thought of this goodness as teleologically and ethically true. "What is truly permanent in human nature is not any condition in which it once existed and from which it has fallen; rather it is the goal for which and toward it moves." Kant looked for constancy, not in what man is, but in what he should be.[60]

Kant had something of great magnitude to say about persons as ends. He wrote:

> Since laws do determine the ends and their general validity, we are able to conceive all ends as constituting a systematic whole of both rational beings as ends in themselves, and of the special ends of each being, if we disregard the personal differentiation of rational beings as well as the content of their private ends. In other words, we can conceive a realm of ends which is possible in accordance with principles stated previously. The reason is that all rational beings are governed by the law that each must treat itself and all other such beings as ends in themselves.[61]

Speaking of Jesus as human, Kant saw him as a great example, and more important for mankind, as human rather than divine. Kant reminded us of what we ought to do:

> When character such as this together with all the afflictions assumed for the sake of the world's highest good, is taken as the ideal mankind, it is by standards of supreme righteousness, a perfectly valid ideal for all men, at all times and in all places, whenever man molds his own character to be like it, as he ought to do. To be sure, such an attainment will ever remain a righteousness not our own, in as much as it would have to consist of a course of life completely and faultlessly harmonious with that perfect character. Yet an appropriation of this righteousness for the sake of our own must be possible when our own character is made similar to that of the archetype. However, the greatest difficulties will stand in the way of our rendering this act of appropriation comprehensible.[62]

This is the Kant of the Age of the Enlightenment speaking. Since every man has a kinship with God by virtue of possessing reason, there is no need for a Christ, the Redeemer. Man makes his own character by its ability to will and live according to universal law.

Brunner

In contrast to Kant, Brunner understands man's relationship to God in transcendental Biblical terms. The God of the Bible is the God who stands over against man. This God is the Creator, who has made himself known in the Word. Man's relationship is to God, not as in Kant through reason and its ability to legislate ethically, but in obedience and love. God made man to live this way, and this is the way he should be understood. Reason regulates in terms of its obedience to the self-revelation of God. The I-self is seen through the divine "Thou." Man's relation to God is to be understood in terms of responsibility. Man's sense of direction comes from his direction from God.[63]

According to Brunner, Kant was the first philosopher in a thousand years to see man as a responsible person, however, this notion of the one, autonomous reason did not let the idea develop. Man became responsible to himself alone and the monistic idea of reason won out.[64]

Man is related to reason and not to God in personal confrontation in Kant's thought. He has a kind of calling, but it is a calling of obligation to the law which he reverences and not to a Creator. Kant recognized the claim on man as a person but ultimately it is not man as a person. The claim comes from man himself and not from the "Thou."[65]

For Brunner, character is "the empirical totality of man as act, understood as a unified act of decision."[66] Character is not primarily emphasized in the Bible, but since it is a middle term between creation and sin, it is important for the Christian. It is the act and choice that precedes particular acts and choices. Character is the deliberate constitution of the self. In a relative sense it is a total act. It is an act that sets the direction and cannot be waved away the next moment with the hand. At the moment of decision, the self determines its constitution.[67]

The decision is unlimited. The self cannot decide to be a dog. It cannot decide to be a saint, reason or no reason aside from faith. This faith must be translated into the concrete history. We have been created by God with good gifts. Man still has the freedom of decision in the daily events of life, but also, and more important, he has freedom to determine his character in faith or righteousness.[68]

Human Evil

Kant

Kant saw man as by nature evil. Man has a bad heart and his choices betray self-love. The wickedness of the human heart comes from neglecting the incentives of maril law in favor of those which "[69]

These are actions which are performed in the consciousness that they are evil actions. This is a use of freedom, and the evil comes from a rule made by the will, which rule is not good. This is misuse of freedom in the will's setting up an evil maxim and cannot be laid to nature, but must be laid to man himself in relation to the moral law. This is not just an individual thing, for this would mean that one man would be good and another bad. This condition cannot be derived from any original act in time. It must be said that this belongs to the will by nature.[70]

Kant pointed out that man in the story of the fall was not bad but betrayed into evil by seduction. Hence, he reasoned that man is capable of becoming better. He started with the proposition that there is nothing in the world good except a good will. He reasoned that the heart may be corrupted, but that the will is good, since it is the agent for man's doing good.[71]

Our morally legislative reason tells us that we ought to do right , therefore, we can do right. Jesus is the archetype of what good really is. He is the perfect example for us to follow, having by his morally legislative will overcome real temptation. Here we may point out that, to Kant, Jesus is not the perfect Son of God who is divine, but a man Jesus who by his achieving has shown us how to live by his use of the practical will to overcome evil.[72] Whereas man had previously attempted to adopt the law of self love along with the moral law, he now uses his will and chooses good maxims in obedience to the moral law.[73] Man originally got off base, so to speak, by choosing a lesser good instead of the highest good. He then questioned the severity of the commandment which demanded good for its own sake without regard for happiness or any other consideration. He finally came to prefer sense impulse over the incentive which sprang from the law, and thus occurred sin. "Man may then be acceptable to God (and so be saved) through a practical faith in this Son of God, so far as He is represented as having taken upon himself man's nature."[74]

Yet Kant will not have help, and assumes man does not need it:

> He and he alone is entitled to look upon himself as an object not unworthy of divine approval who is conscious of such moral convictions as enable him to have a well grounded confidence in himself and to believe that, under like temptations and applications, so far as these are made the touchstone of that idea, he would be loyal unswervingly to the archetype of humanity and by faithful imitation remain true to his example.[75]

Kant saw the true nature of man so clearly that his contemporaries with their predisposition to the optimistic prejudices of the Age of the Enlightenment charged him with hypocrisy and the betrayal of philosophy. Yet, Kant was not really true to his own insight about evil and man, for in the third part of the book, *Religion Within the Limits of Reason*, he backtracked on his earlier insights, lest he go too far. He had to preserve the rational man as good or his whole previous work would be undone. He was able to save his previous work and keep his present insight by the now familiar device of splitting the self into the intelligible self which can overcome evil by its own effort by willing the good, and the empirical self which falls a prey to the seductions of the senses and self-love.[76]

Brunner

According to Brunner, Kant's view is what the reflective man can arrive at by thinking for himself. Brunner's view is, of course, the Reformation's Biblically based view. Man is a sinner and lives in contradiction with what he knows is best for himself, and outside of God he is easily enslaved by the state because he loses his sense of direction and his claim to the innate rights God has willed for him. There has to be a choice between the Kantian or the Brunnerean point of view at this point. There can be no straddling of the fence. The assertion of the autonomy of reason is Pelagian and precludes the Christian teaching on sin and grace.

It is true that the Kantian assertion of the autonomy of reason allows for responsibility. That was the very basis of Pelagius' protest on his visit to Rome. It seemed to him that Augustine's teaching did not arouse the population to real and sufficient moral achievement. Kant asserts his own Pelagian position.[77] However, the assertion of the autonomy of reason does not allow for any feeling for the "Thou."

There is reverence for the law, but the law is impersonal. In one sense it can be said that the law itself comes between man and God to keep man from feeling reverence for the "Thou." The nature of sin produces a sense of alienation which can only be restored by the grace of God conferred in the encounter. It is sufficient that Kant never speaks of sin but of evil. Kant has no understanding that without grace man takes his own life into his own hands, breaks away from God, and desires and claims to do good on his own.[78]

Sin is not weakness, according to Brunner. It is in part the result of weakness; it is mingled with anxiety for one's own life, a fear of losing something by obedience to God. Thus sin is a lack of confidence in God and a fear of venturing all for him. It is not imprudence, but anxiety about oneself. It is not merely rebellion; it is a kind of dizziness which attacks those who ought to step over the abyss leaning only on God. Man's sin consists in believing that he can look after himself better than God can look after him.[79]

Summary

There is a real need for a study of this nature, since legal philosophy has been dominated considerably since the Roosevelt era by sociological jurisprudence. This philosophy has produced some excellent results in the area of legislative achievement, but more transcendental insights are needed to water its drying springs and to insure deeper insights into justice in a world that has seen the emergence of the state as the source of all insight and power.

Kant and Brunner have wrestled with the problems that make for justice in our world; each in his own time had made his contribution. These contributions are not confined to the times these men have lived. Kant attempted to solve the problems of right by his theory of duties. Both his ethics and his legal philosophy are based on the categorical imperative. This means that his legal philosophy is in a sense individualistic.[80] Each man's will to legislate the universal is a part of Kant's teaching, however, there is the aspect of compulsion when anyone abuses the freedom of another.

The key to Brunner's thought is the order of creation. This means that human justice always has the natural law as the basis of its appeal. God's creative ordinance guarantees the right of justice in its own realm, the realm of systems. The law of nature gives to each his due. The law of nature subjects and regulates the instincts of men, whether the instincts be that of power, gain, or sex.

There is no true recognition of justice if there is no recognition of the Creator. The rights of men are the right which God has given. God gives the grace to man to do what he cannot do himself when he seeks the will of God to do it. The relationship of man to God is the image of God rather than a kinship of reason. Real love comes from God and all human love has to be fed at this spring to keep going. Love is living-kindness between persons. Justice has as its domain the systems under which man lives and is summed up in giving to each what is his due.

Endnotes

1. Francis R. Aumann, *The Changing American Legal System, Some Selected Phases*, p. 5.
2. Ibid., p. 6.
3. Edward G. Morgan, *John Winthrop, The Puritan Dilemma*, p. 23.
4. Roscoe Pound, *The Spirit of the Common Law*, p. 40.
5. Pound, *The Spirit of the Common Law*, p. 19.
6. Daniel J. Boorstin, *The Mysterious Science of the Law*, p. 25.
7. Henry Steele Commager, *The American Mind*, p. 359.
8. Ibid., p. 359.
9. James Parker Hall, *American Law and Procedure*, introduction to Volume I, p. xix.
10. Frederick Sass, "Injunctions and Other Equitable Remedies," Lecture 30, *American Law and Procedure*, p. 8.
11. Commager, op. cit., p. 360. Natural law theory of the eighteenth century was being applied to the twentieth century. A change had to come.
12. Ibid.
13. Boorstin, *The Mysterious Science of the Law*, p. 60.
14. Ibid., p. 372.
15. Ibid., p. 373.
16. Loc. cit.
17. Alpheus Mason, Brandeis, *A Free Man's Life*, p. 382.

18. Pound, *The Spirit of the Common Law*, p. 41.
19. Ibid., p. 16.
20. Pound, *An Interpretation of Legal History*, p. 152.
21. Roscoe Pound, *The Spirit of the Common Law*, p. 112.
22. Holmes seems to have been completely indifferent so far as religion is concerned. Cardoza and Brandeis were both Jews. Cardoza was greatly influenced by John Dewey, but was not indifferent to religion. Brandeis became a Zionist in his later years and was always at heart a social reformer.
23. Richard Kroner, *Speculation and Revelation in Modern Philosophy*, p. 224. The moral law is called holy. It seems in Kant to have a transcendent aspect lacking in normal natural law thought.
24. Roscoe Pound, *The Spirit of the Common Law*, p. 8. Pound points out that there is no difference between Kant and Spencer at this point. Spencer's idea came from Kant through Savigny.
25. Huntington Cairns, *Legal Philosophy from Plato to Hegel*, p. 42.
26. Ibid., p. 403.
27. Kant, *The Metaphysics of Morals*, Abbott, translator, p. 150.
28. Kant, *The Philosophy of Law*, p. 42.
29. Ibid., p. 44. Also Gierke, *Natural Law and the Theory of Society*, p. 329.
30. Gierke, *Natural Law and the Theory of Society*, p. 109.
31. Kant, "The Universal Ideal of History" in *The Philosophy of Kant*, Friedrich, editor.
32. Brunner, *Justice and the Social Order*, p. 17.
33. Brunner, *The Divine Imperative*, p. 40. This might raise the question of general revelation, but in that case, the ethic in general revelation would be God's will rather than the principle of the universality.
34. Kant, *The Metaphysics of Morals*, Abbott, translator, p. 140.
35. Kant, *The Metaphysics of Morals*, Abbott, translator, p. 13.
36. Kant, *The Metaphysics of Morals*, Abbott, translator, p. 143.
37. Kant, *The Metaphysics of Morals*, Abbott, translator, p. 147.
38. Ibid., p. 149.

39. Ibid., p. 150.
40. Ibid., p. 161.
41. Kant, *The Metaphysics of Morals*, Abbott, translator, p. 39.
42. Ibid., p. 46.
43. Kant, *The Metaphysics of Morals*, Abbott, translator, p. 206.
44. Brunner, *The Divine Imperative*, p. 46.
45. Ibid., p. 46.
46. Ibid., p. 48.
47. Brunner writes, "It is well known that Kant ultimately came to terms with eudaemonism, in order to reach a material ethic at all, and this, in itself, shows very clearly the fundamental difficulty in his theory." *The Divine Imperative*, p. 49.
48. Ibid., pp. 48-49.
49. Ibid., pp. 54-55.
50. Ibid., p. 59.
51. Ibid., p. 77.
52. Ibid., p. 77.
53. Ibid., p. 77.
54. Ibid., p. 80.
55. Charles W. Hendel, *The Philosophy of Kant*, p. 3.
56. Hendel, op. cit., p. 9.
57. Kant, *Religion Within the Limits of Reason*, p. 398.
58. Hendel, op. cit., p. 3.
59. Kant, *Religion Within the Limits of Reason*, p. 402.
60. Ernst Cassirer, *Rousseau, Kant, Goethe*, p. 20. Unlike many modern thinkers on jurisprudence, Kant did not separate ethics from law. He argued that the theory of law, like that of ethics, is a theory of duties. He thought man should be considered from such a standpoint. His skepticism and his Newtonian theory of cause and effect in the sensible world got him into a difficulty because he knew freedom must be kept. He saw the capacity of freedom as wholly suprasenual and independent of physical phenonema in contra-distinction to his other self which is affected by such deterioration. Also see Gierke, *Natural Law and the Theory of Scoiety, 1500 to 1800*, p. 329.

61. Kant, *The Metaphysicsl of Morals*, Abbott, translator, pp. 181-182.
62. Kant, *Religion Within the Limits of Reason*, Friedrich, editor, p. 402.
63. Brunner, *Man in Revolt*, p. 102.
64. Ibid., p. 100.
65. Ibid., p. 223.
66. Ibid., p. 302.
67. Ibid., p. 305.
68. Ibid., p. 473.
69. Kant, *Religion Within the Limits of Reason*, p. 377.
70. Ibid., p. 3.
71. Ibid., p. 392.
72. Ibid., p. 396.
73. Ibid., p. 384.
74. Ibid., p. 397.
75. Ibid., pp. 397-398.
76. Gierke, *Natural Law and the Theory of Society*, p. 329.
77. Kant, *Religion Within the Limits of Reason*, p. 369.
78. Brunner, *Man in Revolt*, p. 127.
79. Ibid., p. 132.
80. It might be thought that any man is a sample of universal man. The reason is universal in Kant, man is not.

CHAPTER IV

Ancient Thinkers on Justice: Plato Through St. Thomas Aquinas

Pre-Christian Thinkers

Introduction

Roscoe Pound thought that law for the Greeks was originally laid down to keep the peace. With Plato and Aristotle it came to express something of reason and order. In the period of decline of Greece, law was used to preserve the status quo.[1] Cairns believed that the Greeks saw that happiness in the state depended upon the observance of its laws.[2] Furthermore, the Greeks knew the responsibility of its citizenry to see that sound laws were made. Solon, for instance, saw law as allotting impartial spheres to the rich and the poor.

It would seem that Plato was interested in the problem of jurisprudence from the time of the condemnation of Socrates. Throughout his life as a philosopher, his academy continued to give attention to the problems of law. It is possible that Plato was deterred from seeking an active political career in Athens when he witnessed the injustice to Socrates. Even so, he knew he could not escape living in the state and the responsibility that it called forth. Consequently, he gave no small amount of his time trying to think out what the guiding principles of justice should be. His journeys to Sicily to help Dionysius II set his city of Syracuse in order were ventures into active politics. Consequently, he showed to the world that a philosopher ought to be concerned about the practical running of the state.[3]

Plato's *Republic* and his *Laws* were two attempts to set forth what he considered should be the guiding principles of the state. All virtues were to center in the cardinal virtue of justice. Cairns put it this way, "if the philosopher is a king, he will prescribe laws for the state based upon the ideal laws which he has perceived in the world of reality."[4] Since Plato was a great influence intellectually in the formation of the orders in medieval society, it is necessary to examine what he has to say on justice.[5]

By the time Aristotle came along, legal conceptions in outline were laid down. As in so much else he did, Aristotle corrected and laid down a methodology of legal thought that has been influential into modern times, particularly, in Roman Catholic legal thought.[6]

Since Plato and Aristotle were the major thinkers before the Christian era, these two men will be the "representative men" in our consideration of the history of the thought on justice during this time, but Plato and Aristotle serve as our "heroes" and our "representative men," to use Carlyle's phraseology.

Plato

Plato taught that a law is a discovery of reality, or more specifically, it is the true reality with respect to the state. The laws which are representative of this reality will be the best possible laws. This is the point of the discussion of the Athenian in *The Laws*. The Athenian said early in the discussion on the laws for the city he would set up, "Keep watch in case I should enact any law either not tending to goodness at all, or tending only to part of it."[7]

It seems that Plato argued that justice is justice because it accords with his idea of the forms. The just man lives and fulfills his function in the world so far as he is doing the just.[8]

The practical implication of Plato's concern that justice be done is set forth in *The Republic*. At the head of the state will be the philosopher king. He will be the embodiment of reason and good. The artisans, the farmers, and the soldiers will have their place and their function to perform. In the state, harmony is the essence of justice. Taylor has reminded us that the statesmen are to have two characteristics: they are to be scientific thinkers and saints. They may be said to be saints because they ought to embody wisdom, courage, temperance, and justice which may be said to be a summation of the other virtues.[9]

Plato is aware of the chaotic elements that affect a city. Therefore, he wants it not too large, and it ought not to be too near the sea coast so that the bad elements will not be disruptive factors. There is the chaos of the cities in their rivalry with each other. This he described as a "war to the knife." He seemed to realize that there was always this rivalry in the state of nature. The logic might be to set war as the ideal. However, Plato will not have it so. The Athenian does not accept the ideal of victory in war, but rather of victory over the self. The good legislator will legislate to have peace without, and must strive for wisdom from within. Man has to learn the harder virtue of facing pleasures and not giving into them.[10]

The legislator in great measure will be a help to men in their battle with themselves and their attempt to live the good life. He has seen the just, the beautiful, and the good.[11]

Reason is connected with the word for law and should be the guide in the law. Two things are to be considered in law: What pleasure ought to be sought and what pain ought to be avoided. The legislator needs to give consideration to these points in setting up laws and arriving at the proper balance.[12]

Man must be brought under reason and learn to obey. In Athens, no one knows how to obey. Mob rule is the result. There should be a division of sovereignty. The populace should have some say and a monarch or ruler also should have his place. Yet, Aristotle felt that the most efficient government would be a strong "tyrant" who would be young, strong, and intelligent. Yet, Taylor held that Plato thought that in a true constitution the sovereign is God. Justice attends him: to follow God means to be like God who is the true "measure" of all things.[13]

The best type of law is the one in common vogue. It consists of commands and prohibitions. There is the realistic touch that there must be the accompanying penalty for violation. Yet, the legislator will try to enlighten the citizen, so that he will follow the new and good legislation and leave any discontent to the worst element of the citizenry.[14]

One is not surprised to find that sex and marriage played a considerable part in Plato's thought on justice and law in the state. In *The Republic* the guardians are to avoid sex and its pleasure except for producing offspring.[15] Apparently, the ideal for Plato throughout his life was that men should be separated from women except for the time of breeding.[16] But he makes the concession to the flesh in his later life that there may be private homes for the guardians.[17]

Taylor pointed out that, like most non-Christians, there is a tendency in Socrates to underestimate the significance of sex for the whole spiritual life of man. It is true that part of his concern is with the danger of overpopulation in his ideal city, for he suggested that where couples are allowed to live together they ought to be persuaded to abstain from overproduction, but if they did not, then there was the recourse of a new colony.[18] Yet, on the other hand, Plato is concerned that all marriages present offspring, and if they do not after ten years, then they must be dissolved. There are penalties for disobedience.

Both boys and girls are to attend school so that they do not run wild. Of course, there must be the emphasis on mathematics, along with law and astronomy. However, the whole final emphasis in the community is to be the "religious sanction."[19]

Christians have always been impressed by Plato's thought. Some have contended that he came into contact with Hebrew thought in his travels to account for his nobility of thought and living. Although, this theory is not accepted by scholars today, it does illustrate how close his thought comes in some respects to theism as we know it.

Plato was weakest at the point of his understanding of sex and marriage. He did not seem to understand that there was more to sex and marriage than genetics. Also, his state was too regimented. There is more here of similarity to medieval church control than is acceptable to modern Protestants. Even though there are some modifications in *The Laws*, this is not always due to conviction but a giving into human weakness. For instance, in *The Laws* he allows for private estates and houses as a concession to human weakness, but as much to the city as to himself.[20]

Yet, there is the noble about Plato. He spoke of God eternally pursuing the "even tenor of his way," while justice attends him. To follow God is to be like him for he is the measure of all things.[21]

Aristotle

The state exists for the development of the good life according to Aristotle. The quality of the life is important. If it were not, animals and slaves would be as important as the citizen. Those who run the state must take into consideration the virtues and how they can be furthered while the vices are eschewed.[22]

A self-governing community is directed best by law and should be the embodiment of reason. The law is said to be reason defined by the common consent. Legislation should teach virtue, and this can be done if men's lives are regulated by intelligence and the right system. No one likes the discipline of virtue, especially the young. However, they will obey it if it is the law, for most people will obey necessity rather than argument and regimentation rather than what is noble.[23]

Aristotle favored customary laws, not because he is conservative, but because laws are safer than the rule of men and more likely to be obeyed. The established laws are possibly more just than the newly written laws.[24]

The basis of positive law should be a constitution. Laws must be made to suit the constitution and not the other way around. This will keep laws from being arbitrary.[25] Yet, along with this, Aristotle preferred a mixed government. This government was to be aristocratic; not too wealthy but intellectually the elite. The group is to rule by the constitution. They are not to be tyrants.

The constitution cannot enforce the ideal either in virtue or in education. The constitutional requirement is rather to be that of what can be expected of the ordinary person. Aristotle meant this more in terms of the mean between the high, which is unattainable, and the low, which ought to be spurned, than such a measure as the "reasonable man."[26]

Habit plays an important part in Aristotle's thinking. He felt that laws which had the force of habit were the best laws for the state. Laws should have the force of being second nature.[27] Education should be in this direction. Man should come to see that it is not a hardship to live according to the constitution, for it is not his hardship but salvation.[28] Good conduct does not come from feeling or capacity, but rather it must be a settled tendency to act in a certain way. Good conduct does not come from nature, for, if it did, man would be in difficulty. He would not be able to change morally. Yet, it is in the very doing of the just and the temperate that men become just and temperate. Aside, from habituation, there would be no prospect of doing good.[29]

This habituation is from within. According to Aristotle, men do not acquire virtue through the help of external goods, but rather they acquire external goods by the help of virtue. This means that one has as much happiness as he has virtue and wisdom. Men are happy by means of their own nature rather than by external good.[30]

The happiness of the individual is the same as the happiness of the state. The wise man and the wise state will both regulate their actions to the best end.[31] Yet, this is not a depreciation of law, for law is accepted reason. Aristotle wrote:

> Therefore he who bids the law rule may be deemed to bid God and Reason alone rule, but he who bids man rule adds an element of the heart, for desire is a wild beast, and passion perverts the minds of rulers, even when they are the best of men. The law is reason unaffected by desire.[32]

W. D. Ross is right in pointing out that with all his zeal for the state Aristotle is free from the delusion which puts the state above morality. He does not treat the state as having a peculiar set of moral values, more accommodating than those which bind individuals. The state is then a moral agent to further the moral life of the individual.[33]

Aristotle offers men an overly rationalized view of who should rule in the state. A too narrow clique who are not too wealthy but are possessed of sufficient reason are to rule.

The Christian would question the adequacy of the golden mean as an adequate method of arriving at ethical decision. Certainly, Aristotle was too prone to use reason to justify the status quo in the area of slavery. Ultimately, criticism has to go back to his religious monism with an implicit dualism in his doctrine of form and matter to show the final inadequacies of his system. It is doubtful that Aristotle's ethics are adequately sustained by his view of a god who is indifferent to the world. Habituation, the Christian sees, has to be preceded by conversion to finally have an adequately enforceable justice.

Yet Plato and Aristotle are noble thinkers. It is easy to see why the more irenic Christians of the past have been reluctant to place them in hell. Zwingli at least seems to have made room in his system for them to be included among the elect. He did this by allowing those who had been born before Christ, and who consequently could have had no chance to know Him to be included among the elect if they had lived the right kind of lives.[34]

St. Thomas: Major Voice of a Medieval Catholic

Introduction

The Stoics early held that men should live in accordance with a single harmonious principle in accordance with universal law. The idea developed of a "true law." There was a divine law in contrast to the laws of a particular state. Thus justice is from something eternal, which rules the whole universe by its wisdom, command, and prohibition.[35]

The true law is right reason: it agrees with nature. It is diffused through all the world and through all men. It is unchanging and universal. It summons to duty by its commands, and deters from wrong by its prohibitions. It is not possible to annul this law, nor can any governing body or people free man from obedience. Those who do not obey abandon their better selves.[36] Thus the divine mind is the supreme law. When reason is perfected in man, that is law as well. This perfected law exists in the mind of wise men.[37]

It may be that Cicero, and certainly there were other Romans besides Cicero who did this, realized something of the mobility of this thought in living, but the letters of Cicero show something of the schemer and the thoroughgoing politician without any serious scruples when it suited his purpose.[38]

The Christian thinkers did not hesitate for long to take the classical thinkers and their work on the law of nature to use it for their own purposes. By the law of nature the early thinkers meant the order of creation. They knew their use of the notion was different from the classical one. Yet, it seemed to be a most useful concept and went to the heart of the matter so far as they were concerned. It expressed the right which proceeded from the God who created the nature of man.[39]

The law of nature was important to justice, because the whole concern for justice was founded upon the notion. The whole idea of justice was founded upon the divine ordinance. This was what gave law the ring of holiness and genuine validity.

The major thinkers took the notion and used it as it best fit into their systems. The great thinker of the medieval period, St. Thomas, was concerned to set forth what justice meant, and, therefore, he used the idea of the law of nature as it related to his idea of the Fall, nature, and grace. He was able to do this by his two-story construction of nature and grace. The Fall chopped off, as it were, grace but did not affect seriously the realm of nature.

Aquinas used Aristotle a great deal as a basis for his thought in realm of nature. These were the four cardinal virtues men could know by reason and could perform without the help of grace. Since, the reason was held to be uncorrupted by the Fall, contrary to what it was stated to have been in Augustine and later in Luther and Calvin, it is easy to see that St. Thomas had the way clear to use the previous thought on natural law, both pre-Christian and Christian. Since reason could by reasoning arrive at a personal God, though it could not know him in his mystery and as he is know in Jesus Christ, it would not be hard to see how reason could deduce positive law from natural law. It is well for us to examine what Aquinas has to say on the nature of justice, law, and the state.

Kinds of Law

Law is for St. Thomas ordained for the common good. The word derives its meaning from "ligere" which means to bind. Therefore, law binds men to act for the common good. Reason served to help accomplish this end. It is the duty of the sovereign to set up ways of promulgation of the law so that the citizenry can obey it and the common good be achieved.[40]

There are four kinds of law according to St. Thomas: the eternal law, the natural law, the human law, and the divine law. God is the divine ruler of the universe, and his rule has the nature of law. Therefore, since this law is not subject to time but is eternal, this kind of law must be called the eternal law. Natural law is man's participation in the divine law. The latter seems to be the imprint of the divine light upon us whereby we know good from evil. Natural law, then is the rational creature's participation in the divine law. Natural law is discovered by examining the eternal law.[41] To the extent that man attains natural law, he is participating in the eternal law.[42] Human laws are the particular laws drawn by human reason from the natural law. There laws are to be deduced by the reason for the particular time and place.[43] The divine law is made up of precepts from the Old and New Testaments.[44]

St. Thomas asked the natural question whether laws are supposed to make men good. He answered that a law is a dictate of reason and is written to be obeyed by those who are subject to it. The effect of law is to lead its subjects to their proper virtue. Of course, a virtue is good, therefore, the effect of law should be good if the ruler had the intention to frame a good law.[45]

The eternal law is the divine wisdom directing all actions and movements. All laws in so far as they partake of right reason are derived from the eternal law. Whatever is subject to divine government is subject to the eternal law. This means that all human beings are subject to the eternal law in that in natural knowledge the mind furnished the light, and grace gives the added knowledge of faith and wisdom in the supernatural realm. The bad are subject to the eternal law in that they fail to obey it.[46]

The natural law is more the eternal law seen from man's side. It is the rational participation on the eternal or the emanation from the eternal to the rational creature. The practical reason is founded upon the notion of good. Reason finds the first precept of the law that good is to be done and evil avoided. All other precepts of the natural law are based on this one, that which is good is to be done and evil avoided. This seeking the good is, also, characteristic of his nature.[47]

It seems that for Aquinas all virtues are prescribed by the natural law, since each man's reason dictates that he should act virtuously as according to nature and the nature of the practical reason.[48]

When the question was raised as to whether natural law is immutable or not, St. Thomas answered that natural law is immutable. The speculative reason is concerned only with what is necessary. Reason is concerned with contingent matters and the more the descent is made to the particular, the more deviation there is. Speculative reason is the same to all men both as to principles and conclusions. The same thing does not hold with particulars. The truth is the same for all men; but practically it is not known equally by all. This is because men have let their reason be distorted by bad habits, by passion, and by bad natural relations.

Natural law can be changed in two ways. It can be added to, for things of benefit to mankind have been added over and above the natural law, both by the divine law and by human law. It can be changed by subtraction, so that what was previously according to natural law is no longer so. Primary principles cannot be changed, but secondary principles can be changed in detail.[49]

The State and Human Law

Natural law is written in the hearts of men. Natural law in the abstract cannot be blotted out. It is, however, blotted out in particular actions in so far as reason is kept from applying the general principles to a particular point of practice.[50]

Human law has just so much of the law of nature as is derived from this same law. But, at any point it defects from the law of nature, it is no longer a law but a perversion of law.[51] Yet, at the same time, human law does not prescribe concerning all virtues but only those virtues that are ordainable to common good. The point is that all that law prescribes which prescribes too much is unenforceable.[52]

The sovereign is not subject to the law but he ought to obey the law voluntarily. The Christian does not have to obey a bad law except to avoid a scandal or disturbance. St. Thomas pointed, particularly, to laws including idolatry or things forbidden in the divine law. In such cases, men must obey God rather than men.[53]

Forms of Government

Men are so busy with their own self-interest that most of them would be in trouble if they had the authority to do the commanding. This is the function of the state. The state rests upon human law. This dominion came through the "ius gentium" which is human law.[54] The rulership comes ultimately from God, but the particular form of government is deduced from the natural law.[55]

Although St. Thomas considered other possibilities for governing, his general references are to a ruler who is above the law.[56] The argument seems to be the logical one, namely that unity is more likely to come from one than many. It would appear that a temperate people can rule themselves. In other places, Aquinas suggested a mixed government. He pointed to Moses and the seventy-two that helped him and his successors rule. He saw the rule of Moses as that of a kingship. The seventy-two were elected; therefore, there was a democratic government to that extent.[57]

All emperors and rulers have their proper sphere, but there is a higher sphere, namely, the spiritual. Consequently, all rulers are subject to the successor of St. Peter, the Vicar of Christ, even as they are subject to the Lord Jesus Christ. "Secular power is subject to the spiritual power as the body is subject to the soul. It is not an assumption of power if the spiritual prelate interferes in temporal things, provided the interference is in those matters where the secular power is subject to him."[58]

Justice

St. Thomas started his discussion on "legal justice" with a quotation from Isadore which states the proposition that justice is giving each his right. A man is just when he respects the rights of others. He reinterpreted the above definition to include his psychology of habit. Then the definition of justice is seen to be thus: justice is a habit whereby a man renders to each his due by a constant and perpetual will.[59] Justice carries with it a certain kind of equality. It has a directive power over virtue and its end achieved is said to be just or right.[60]

Legal justice is classified as a general virtue, and it directs all other virtues to its own end. The end it has is to move all other virtues to its own end. Legal justice directs men to the common good. However, there is need for other virtues to direct immediately to particular goods. These virtues may be directed toward me, myself, or toward other men. The virtues which are concerned about my relationship with myself and with right are internal virtues; those concerned with the external are legal virtues and are the subject of justice. The legal virtues consist in relegating what is due to each according to equality of proportion. In other words, the aim of justice is to render to each what belongs to him.[61]

Criticism

There can be no question but that the Thomistic theory of justice has exerted a great influence and still exerts great influence today. It must be said that not all of it is good from the Biblical and Protestant Christian points of view.

Reinhold Niebuhr has criticized the social ethics of St. Thomas for embodying the peculiarities and the contingent factors of a feudal economy and writing them into natural law.[62] He, further, criticized Thomism for the "preamble" to its natural law which lays down things as they should be to accomplish good and not to accomplish evil.[63]

Brunner said something of the same thing when he criticized the Thomistic position for its formulated law, for it amounts to the law of nature being in competition with the law of the state. There is danger to the state that is related to a church with a prescriptive moral or natural law which invalidates positive law where there is a disagreement. This is the place where a Protestant view of the law of nature differs most definitely from medieval and modern Catholicism. "The Protestant view of the law of nature can only reveal the injustice of the decree of the state; it cannot release the citizen from the duty of obeying that unjust decree."[6]

However, when the state makes itself God or fosters idolatry, there can be no doubt that the Christian will rise to throw off the false gods. Otherwise, the order of creation with its guarantee that there is such a thing as absolute justice would be worthless.

Endnotes

1. Pound, *Introduction to the Philosophy of Law*, p. 35.
2. Cairns, *Legal Philosophy from Plato to Hegel*, p. 31.
3. A. E. Taylor, *Plato: The Man and His Work*, p. 7.
4. Cairns, *Legal Philosophy from Plato to Hegel*, p. 36.
5. Taylor does not draw this conclusion exactly, but he does draw the analogy. "His rulers are much more in the position of medieval military order than in that of a collectivist bureaucracy, Op. cit., p. 277.
6 One may not agree with Aristotle, but some neo-Thomists follow rather closely his methodology at many points.
7. Plato, *The Laws*, p. 705.
8. Plato, *The Republic*, p. 354.
9. Taylor, *Plato: The Man and His Work*, p. 283.
10. Ibid., p.. 468-469.
11. Cairns, *Legal Philosophy from Plato to Hegel*, p. 44.
12. Plato, *The Laws*, p. 744a.
13. Taylor, op. ċit., p. 474.
14. Ibid., p. 472.
15. Plato, *The Republic*, p. 415.
16. Plato, *The Laws*, p. 740.
17. Taylor, *Plato: The Man and His Work*, p. 481.
18. Plato, *The Laws*, p. 740.
19. Ibid., p. 828.
20. Ibid., p. 479.
21. Ibid., p. 474.
22. Aristotle, *Politics*, 1280 b 5.

23. Aristotle, *Nicomachean Ethics*, 1180 a.
24. Aristotle, *Politics*, 1287 a.
25. Ibid., 1294 a 20.
26. Ibid., 1294 25. The concept of the "reasonable man" is the common law measure-to-measure liability in civil suits. It is used also in criminal suits to determine the degree of punishment. In either case the measure is the ordinary man with average reasoning capacity. In civil suits, the measure is the ordinary competence in the class the defendent holds himself out to be able to perform.
27. Ibid., 1287 25.
28. Aristotle, *Politics*, 1287 a.
29. Aristotle, *Nicomachean Ethics*, 1105 b, 10. It is at this point that Protestants differ from Aristotle, St. Thomas, and John Dewey greatly. Conversion has to be prior religiously to good habit.
30. Aristotle, *Politics*, 1323 b 25.
31. Ibid., 1324 a 30.
32. Ibid., 1286 b 30.
33. W. D. Ross, *Aristotle*, p 280.
34. Lecture notes, based on Dr. Ernest Stoeffler's course on lectures, "Major Voices of the Reformation," Temple University, January, 1958.
35. Cairns, *Legal Philosophy from Plato to Hegel*, p. 135.
36. Ibid., p. 138.
37. Ibid., p. 139.
38. Cicero, *Letters*, particularly those which deal with Julius Caesar.
39. Brunner, *Justice and the Social Order*, p. 84.
40. Aquinas, *Summa Theologica*, 1:1 Q. 90.
41. Ibid., 1:11 Q. 91, Art. 2.
42. Ibid., 1:11 A. 91, Art. 4.
43. Ibid., 1:11 A. 91, Art. 3
44. Ibid., 1:11 A. 91, Art. 5.
45. Ibid., 1:11 A. 92, Art. 1.
46. Ibid., 1:11 A. 94
47. Ibid., 1:11 A. 94, Art. 2.

48. Ibid., 1:11 A. 94, Art. 3.
49. Ibid., 1:11 A. 94, Art. 5.
50. Ibid., 1:11 A. 94, Art. 6.
51. Ibid., 1:11 A. 95, Art. 2.
52. Ibid., 1:11 A. 95, Art. 3.
53. Ibid., 1:11 Q. 95, Art. 4; the appeal is to Acts 5:29.
54. Ibid., 1:11 Q. 12, Art. 2.
55. Ibid., 1:11 Q. 94, Art. 5.
56. Ibid., 1:11 Q. 95, Art. 3.
57. Ibid., 1:11 Q. 105.
58. Ibid., 11:11 Q. 60, Art. 6.
59. Ibid., 11:11, Q. 58, Art. 1.
60. v11:11, Q 57, Art. 1.
61. Ibid., 11:11, Q 65.
62. Niebuhr, *The Nature and Destiny of Man*, Vol I., p. 281.
63. Niebuhr, *Christian Realism and Political Problems*, p. 148
64. Brunner, *Justice and the Social Order*, p. 38.

CHAPTER V

Modern Thinkers on Justice: Calvin to Laski

INTRODUCTION

So far as Protestant thought is concerned, it received its most thorough systemization and its highest polish in John Calvin's *Institutes of the Christian Religion*. This statement is true so far as theology is concerned, but it is not true of his concern for the state and legal justice. Here Calvin reflected St. Augustine more exactly than in other places. However, Calvin did have great influence for political enlightenment and moral and religious transformation. His holy city Geneva was the fruit of his preaching.

Man, in Calvin's thought, has fallen into corruption, but this fall was not so thoroughgoing that men could not be under common grace. Although, man's reason has been affected by the fall, he still can set up systems of justice according to the law of nature or the moral law.[1]

In England in 1651, there was a book published that was of quite a different calibre, although, it too was well written. The author's pessimism was more complete than that of Calvin, because he saw no resolution of his pessimism. Whereas Calvin had written to tell of the sovereignty of God, Hobbes developed a materialistic metaphysics which left no room for human individuality. His individuals are animals with a strong impulse to survival.[2]

It was not Hobbes's metaphysics but his idea of social contract which became popular with pessimists. He saw the social contract as the means of bringing peace out of a state of nature which was a war of all against all. He saw the sovereign as absolute, since this was the only way "the war to the knife" could be brought to an end.

It has been said that Rousseau was a sentimental deist with more sentimentality than deism. What is so surprising is that he came out of Geneva, the home of Calvinism. At one time, he was, also, a Roman Catholic, but in reality his thought was acceptable to neither Protestant nor Catholic orthodoxy. His voice was raised against the evils of society. Rousseau thought the answer was in a good human nature restored to its happy state of nature. The social contract had been set up originally that men might make the fullest use of their rights and exercise their authority through the general will.

Hegel was a professor in the University of Berlin at the time when Germany was feeling the surge of the nationalist spirit. He became the spokesman for the concept of an absolute Spirit which was becoming conscious of itself. This Spirit could be best seen in the state, which was God marching through history.

Eventually, Karl Marx stood Hegel's logic on its head and gave to materialism an inherent dialectic. The proleteriat is destined to rule by this inherent destiny. Law and all the instruments of government are the tools of the class in power but will be snatched by the working class for a like use in their dictatorship. Harold Laski actually makes a better subject of study than Marx, because in both America and Great Britain he was so widely read in the 1930s and 1940s. For him, the Marxian revolution was inevitable, because it was just that labor should come into its own.

Calvin

Perhaps, some students are most surprised to find that Calvin taught the doctrine of natural law. The reason one is surprised is that he has heard so much about Calvin's doctrine of total corruption and his general pessimism. However, Calvin is clear in his teaching on natural law. He equated natural law with moral law, which has been engraved by God on the minds of men. The content of this law is equity which is the same for all mankind. This equity must be the scope and rule of all laws. Having this equity of the moral law is sufficient. However, legislators, like Moses of old, have to take into account the particular circumstance of a particular time.[3] Far from being obedient to the natural law, as Calvin advised, there are some Christians who think they can disregard the laws of God himself, do away with all law and live only in obedience to Christ himself. They think they can individualistically enjoy their Christian liberty. They think nothing is good unless they have something new. They disregard magistrate and king. But Calvin pointed out firmly that people of this mind do not understand that there is a difference between spiritual liberty and political obedience. It is the difference between the body and the soul, of the present life and eternal life. All this Christian liberty must be confined within its proper limits.[4] Yet, it is important to note that each is proper within its own sphere, and there is no variance with the other.

Calvin held that the civil government has as its function to further the worship of God and the doctrines of the church, to regulate our lives in a proper manner so that civil justice may be carried out, and to establish general peace and tranquility. Some men imagine that perfection can be found in human communities, but they do not understand that men, exercising their purported Christian liberty in the community would perpetrate all kinds of crimes with impunity.[5]

Much of Calvin's treatise on "Civil Government" could take for its text the well-known passage, "There is no power but of God; the powers that be are ordained of God. Rulers are ministers of God, revengers to execute wrath upon him that doeth evil. Do that which is good, and thou shalt have praise for the same."[6]

The magistrates have, according to Calvin, their command from God; they have authority and are his representatives and act as his vicegerents. Consequently, there should be no doubt that the civil magistracy is a calling legitimate, honorable, and holy.[7]

Calvin did not hesitate to admit that he preferred an aristocratic government or a mixture of aristocracy and democratic elements. Whichever way the government is set up, the magistrate must do his duty to keep things under control, but also, the people must remember that whether the government be that of a king ruling, a magistrate, or whatever be God's pleasure the people must be obedient to any governor God appoints.[8]

Calvin believed in the lawfulness of wars to avenge public wrongs, however, this practice should be kept as a last measure and not resorted to lightly. Yet, he reasoned, the prince should not be given power to punish individual crimes within the realm without having the right to defend the realm from the outside enemies.[9]

Princes have the right, Calvin pointed out, to collect taxes, tribute, and legitimate revenues. Princes have to live according to their station, and the money has to come fairly from their subjects. Yet, the princes ought to remember that the moneys they have to spend are not so much private income as revenue from the people.[10]

The moral law requires men to worship with faith and piety and to love other men with sincere love, but there is, also, given the judicial law. This is given as a political contribution so that men learn to do justice and live peaceably with one another.[11]

The Anabaptists of Calvin's time were taking seriously the passage about nonresistance: if anyone smite you on one cheek, turn the other, and if one takes you to law to get thy coat, give him thy cloak, also. To them it meant that no Christian should go to law.[12] Calvin pointed out that if hate were the motive, it would be wrong to go to court, but if the desire was to get the affair settled in fairness and Christian understanding, then it would be perfectly all right to go to court.[13]

By all odds, the most important of Calvin's teachings on civil government was wrung from him reluctantly. The political events in France, Holland, Scotland, and England made it tremendously important. Whereas Lutheranism gained the reputation for being entirely submissive to the prince, Calvinism became the spearhead of resistance for better and more popular government. After all, the exhortation of obedience to magistrates and those in authority, Calvin made this exception: If the magistrate should try to keep men from being obedient to God and should actively work to seduce Christians away from their faith, then it becomes necessary to offer resistance. It would be foolish to secure the pleasure of men and at the same time bring down the displeasure of God. "We must obey God rather than men" becomes the battle cry under the circumstances.[14] The Christians have to disregard the command of the magistrate in such a circumstance.[15]

Calvinism

Hotman

When the French Calvinists got into difficulty because of their Protestant faith and were undergoing severe persecution, they wrote to Calvin for advice. For a long time, he advised submission and endurance, but finally he did allow resistance if the situation became unbearable.

One of the French Calvinists was interested in the problem put to Calvin, and he did a great deal of work to direct Calvinism in its struggles. Hotman attempted to prove by history that a general assembly of nations had exercised high political powers. He sought to prove that monarchy was limited by the people, by the estates, and by constitutional law. Ruler and subject were bound by contract, but if the ruler breaks his part of the contract the people were justified in rebelling. It can be seen that Hotman was more interested in political theory than Calvin. He was a lawyer as reflected in his reverence for precedent and law.[16]

As would be expected, he raised the question as to whether a ruler should be obeyed when he commands contrary to the laws of God. He naturally gave a negative answer. He used Scripture and the analogy of a feudal lord to prove his point. The serf is released from his contract when the liege lord first broke it. So the people were released from their contract with their ruler when he broke his contract with the people.[17] If the king did not keep his contract, the people need not either. However, the resistance had to be by assemblies or magistrates and not by the common citizen. He, further, argues for popular sovereignty on the ground that the people went into the contract and voluntarily created political institutions, therefore, when the contract was voided, they were free to choose what government they would.[18]

Knox

John Knox of Scotland was a great preacher, but he had little concern for legal philosophy as such. He enunciated in dramatic form the legal principle that the lower nobility may revolt if driven to it by the danger of Catholicism. The most feared danger was that Catholicism would be restored as the religion of the state. This would have meant that Mary Stuart, today called Mary Queen of Scots, her unruly following, her hated French friends, and the Catholic church would have been in control. Knox would have none of this, however, for he had already suffered for the Protestant cause. He had spent three years already as a galley slave because he was a Protestant.

When Mary returned to Scotland a queen, Knox was the leader of the opposition. He was summoned on three different occasions, possibly for Queen Mary to see if she could win him to her cause, or at least to lessen his opposition. In Knox's first interview with Queen Mary, she asked him, "Think ye that subjects, having the power, may resist their princes?"

Knox replied, "If their princes exceed their bounds, Madam; no doubt they may be resisted, even by power."

He is then asked about the right to assert his Kirk as over against hers when she thinks the Roman Catholic Church is the true church.

Knox replied, "Ye shall believe that God plainly speaketh in his Word... The World of God is plain in itself."[19]

Knox seemed to be going in the direction of Hotman, though doubtless this was not his full intent. Yet, this is a part of a later interview with Queen Mary.

"Who are you," the Queen asked, "that presume to school the nobles and sovereign of this realm?"

"Madam," Knox replied, "a subject born within the same."[20]

Knox was asserting that the lesser nobility and the magistrates might overthrow the sovereign. Mary seemed to be leading the nation into idolatry again in attempting to restore Catholicism with its statues of the Virgin Mary and the saints.

Puritanism

Colonel John Lilbourne was ahead of many of his fellow Puritans when he advocated the sovereignty of the common people and maintained that Parliament was the agent of the nation as a whole.[21]

John Milton believed that laws consented to by all bound the rulers as well as the subjects. The people had ultimate political power, and they could depose a king as well as establish him. As a matter of fact, he thought people were under the obligation to remove tyrants.[22]

Another Puritan contribution was the idea of the holy commonwealth with its emphasis on having a church of saints. The saints were to furnish the ideals and the seal to make a holy commonwealth possible.

Much against their wishes, the Puritans were responsible through persecution for helping Roger Williams develop his thought of a free church in a free state. Doubtless the persecution helped Williams to see the value of toleration. Consequently, he accepted all who wished to settle in Rhode Island, the colony Williams developed.[23]

Thomas Hobbes

Oakeshott thought *Leviathan* by Hobbes was the greatest masterpiece of political philosophy ever written in the English language.[24] If this be so, it is because of the excellence of the composition and not because the ideas of the author could ever be acceptable to those who are interested in founding a Christian society. It is interesting that Kant knew Hobbes's work and thought him important enough to refute, particularly, at the point of the relevance of constitutional law.[25]

Before there was any law, Hobbes asserts, when men lived in a state of nature, there was a war of all against all. There may not have been actual fighting at all times, but there was always the attitude of war. There was no justice; fraud and force were the cardinal virtues. There was no property; no mine and thine, but only what each man could get for himself.[26]

Passion and reason became dissatisfied with this condition. The passions that inclined men were fear of death, desire of such things as are necessary to commodious living, and a hope that by industry they could obtain them. Human reason followed the lead of the passions and suggested articles of peace which men might live by, and set to itself the task of drawing up an agreement.[27]

Man gave up the right to hinder others in what they had. This was easy in that he only gave up what he did not have a right to in the first place. He transferred this power to a sovereign power. This transfer was in return for some benefit to himself. This mutual transferring of rights is called contract.

Men agreed upon this transfer of rights for benefits and made the contract without the sovereign being present to contract it. The contract was delivered to him later.[28] Upon acceptance by the sovereign, the contract was in force. The sovereign was to keep the peace. Man henceforth would be in awe of the sovereign because of his great power. The sovereign was to direct the actions of all men in the state for their common benefit henceforth.

Since the sovereign was not a party to the contract when it was originally drawn, he is above it. He has it as his due and those who draw the contract are said to merit what they receive from him. This is an abiding agreement and not to be broken by those who gave up their rights, nor can the sovereign upon his acceptance give up his rights. However, he may delegate power.[29]

Hobbes had the lawyer's natural inclination to make distinctions.

To him the sovereign is not just another person. He is a corporated person. That would not solve anything. He is the representative of each man. This representative has to be an artificial person: he is the one who impersonates a number of natural persons. The covenant then institutes an office which may be held by one man or by an assembly of men, but which is distinct from the natural person of the holder. This artificial person becomes possessed of authority to act, and will action for each separate man.[30]

Hobbes had no doubt that the best sovereign was the monarch, for then there would be no struggle for power. He would be in complete control. However, it is important to recognize that this is not the only kind of government he considers. Whether the sovereign be one person or an assembly, he (or they) is exempt from control of the law in so far as he may change it, but not in the sense that he need not obey it while it is in force.[31]

The positive law and the law of nature contain each other and are of equal extent. The laws of nature are not properly laws, but are qualities that dispose men to peace. These qualities are equity, justice, gratitude, and other moral virtues depending on these. They become laws when the commonwealth is settled, and they are made law by the will of the sovereign. On the other hand, the civil law is part of the dictates of nature, for justice is the performance of the covenant—the giving each his due. This dictate is a dictate of the law of nature. The sovereign, in other words, ought to perform his duty by giving equity. However, every subject has covenanted to obey the civil law and this is a part of the law of nature.[32] It must be remembered that the sovereign is in complete control until he no longer furnished protection, orders the states and keeps the enemy out.[33]

According to Hobbes, it is the right of the sovereign to determine the content of religion within the state. However, this seems to apply only to public worship; yet, the sovereign is the head of the church as well as the state.[34]

Brunner criticized Hobbes for his emphasis on egoism as the only motive for action and for his Epicureanism. Hobbes' concept of the state is not based on goodwill but on fear. The state and civilization may be explained as the result of fear of one another.[35]

Rousseau

Kendell reminded his readers in his "Introduction" to *The Social Contract* not to expect a book that was free of inconsistencies and contradictions. Doubtless the weaknesses of the book have been in some sense its strengths as seen from the variety of people it has influenced, two among many being Kant and Tolstoi.[36]

One could scarcely expect consistency from a man who was a wanderer over Europe, at one time a Protestant, then a Catholic, then a Protestant, again, and perhaps most of the time neither. He was once a friend of D'Alembert and David Hume and later their bitter enemy. His morals were anything but responsible and at times he bordered on the paranoia in his suspicion of just about every one in his later years.[37]

Rousseau was a spokesman for equality. He believed that men were everywhere in slavery, when they were meant to be free. It should have been that the equality that was present when the social contract was drawn was meant to carry on man's essential equality with other men.[38]

That Rousseau was no apostle of tradition can be seen in the way he handled legal tradition. He said, "Learned studies of public law are often merely histories of ancient abuses; and those who devote hard study to them are misdirecting their energies."[39] Society, Rousseau stressed, was organized by a social contract. This is the only way society could be ordered. Agreement and consent are necessary for any sovereign to exercise authority. This purportedly would be the way liberty would be retained, for in becoming a member of the group and obeying the general will man is only obeying himself, and so he remains free as before.[40]

With the advancement of civilization, social barriers have arisen. Some people have become rich and more have become poor. The strong have taken advantage of their strength and some men have become slaves under these strong men as masters. The masters have tried to justify their position, but granted that although a man could alienate his rights and be a slave, he could not alienate the rights of his children.[41]

Slavery and right cannot keep house together. The individual gave his rights to the community as a whole. Far from being a slave or unequal, each person possesses an equal and inalienable portion of the sovereignty of the whole.

The authority given in the contract does not negate individual rights. His doctrine of the general will is important at this point. The individual will finds its fullest expression and the guarantee of its own rightness in the general will. In voting this normally means the vote of the majority ought to be followed, however, the majority is not absolutely identified with the general will. The general will could not be wrong by definition, since it is the general will and, therefore, the interest of the community. A test of the realized general will is the prospering of the community.[42]

Rousseau believed that the majority vote was normally the best method of arriving at the general will. He preferred a small state to a large one so that on a set day all the people could get together and give their sanction to the constitution. Officers were to be elected on that day as well. The general bolstering of the sovereignty of the state is the chief purpose of getting together.[43]

According to Rousseau, the general will was being realized when all went well in the assembly. Where there was wrangling and bickering, particular interests were attempting to assert their will over the general will. However, he was careful to point out that a too general agreement could mean that a people had sold themselves into slavery or were being swayed by intimidation or flattery.[44]

It appears that Rousseau allowed a simple ethical religion of the "Gospel," but he did not feel that religion would make any contribution to the laws and obedience to them. Rather the laws were to be worked up without any consideration for the Christian religion.[45] There is to be a religion of duty to the state, and in this respect Rousseau praised Hobbes for having wisdom enough to subordinate religion to the state.[46] The sovereign is entitled to fix the tenets of a purely civil creed or profession of faith. These would not be dogmas, but sentiments deemed indispensable for participating in the state. The state would, in short, regulate morality and the duties that each person has to discharge toward others. Aside from these things, each person can hold what opinion he pleases. "Let the citizens be good citizens in this life, and their fate in the life to come—be that fate what it may—is no affair of the sovereign's."[47]

The social contract was germinal. It might have been expected that its obvious sentimentality would have prevented its widespread use, but such was not the case. It influenced Marxian thought, to cite but one example.

Rousseau's "general will" is a dangerous concept, unless some means are taken to protect the minority. Hitler was put into power by the general will, for he came into power constitutionally. The emphasis on the goodness of man was a failure to take into consideration any of the Christian teaching with its realistic evaluation of man and his state.

Hegel on the State and Law

Hegel's philosophy is governed by the most abstract principles, yet, it seems to demonstrate that once ideas are thrown out into the world, one can never be sure what their effect will be. His thought on the state will be discussed here, since it has had the most practical and tragic results through Marxism even into our time.

The state is the cosmic Spirit that lives in the world and realizes itself in it consciously, while in nature the spirit is known as the other or is dormant only. Spirit is really conscious of itself in the state. In fact, the state is "the march of God through the world." The Spirit is realizing itself as will. Hegel was careful to say that no particular state can be considered God himself. Evil may mar this God but it cannot take away his goodness, for the affirmative persists in spite of defects. "We must, therefore, worship the state as the manifestation of the divine on earth."[48] The state is an organism, or the development of the idea into differences. Hegel means here that in the constitution the different powers and different functions are made explicit. The state maintains itself through the constitution. The relation of the constitution to the state is one of an organism. If the two different sides of the same thing—the constitution and the state—get separated, it is like different organs of the body failing to work together and sickness results.

The complete state has, according to Hegel, complete consciousness and thought. The state knows what it wills and it wills it under the form of thought.[49] This organism, also, includes religion. The organization of the state is concerned with the external aspects of life and religion with the internal. Trouble develops when, for instance, the church becomes concerned with the external, which is the prerogative of the state.[50] Hegel said elsewhere that the state and laws are the manifestation of religion on earth.[51] It seems that the state and religion have a perfect relationship in Protestantism.[52] It was through the Reformation that freedom came to full consciousness.[53]

The constitution is rational in so far as it defines the state and its functions according to the nature of its concept. The principle of the constitution is, therefore, absolutely perpetual, divine, substantial, and above and beyond the sphere of what is made. The constitution is not just a thing; it is the work of centuries. It is the idea and the consciousness of what is rational in so far as it is developed in people. A constitution is not made by people, but it must be felt to be the embodiment of the right. Right is thought upon and in time passes into general consciousness, and then presumably is given effect in a constitution.[54]

There is evidence that Hegel became more conservative when he grew older. In any case, in the works here considered Hegel takes a very conservative viewpoint.

Hegel considered other types of state organization, but he reasoned that a people without its monarch and without the organization that goes with him is a formless mass, which no longer belongs to the state.[55] This is not to say that Hegel did not believe in the division of powers into the executive and the legislative branches of the government. He saw the executive branch as made up of hard-working civil servants which go to make up in part the middle class. The legislative branch is to stick to the meaning of the constitution in its legislation.[56]

While Kant and Brunner, as will be seen later, both wrote in the hope of eliminating war, Hegel wrote unto the glorification and justification of war. He taught that by war the health of nations was to be preserved. History also shows that wars have checked unrest and generally strengthened the state by quieting unrest.[57]

The military class is the class of universality. Its function is to guard the state, and this is its privilege. It needs to realize the ideality of such sacrifice. The chief virtue is self-subordination to the universal cause. Modern warfare has made the group and its work more important than the individual with his individual deeds. Therefore, group achievement is to be sought and praised.[58]

Hegel criticized Kant for his thought on eternal peace and his desire to set up a federation of nations. He saw each state as an individual and as, essentially, self-contained. There might be a federation, but the danger is implicit that other states will form an alliance to counterbalance it.[59]

He saw each state as existing largely for itself. It might be interested to know what was going on in other states but only in terms of protection for itself. Yet all this turmoil is not bad, for out of this conflict of nations with their finite spirits comes the universal Spirit, pronouncing its judgment upon the finite of the world's history: "For the history of the world is the world's court of justice."[60]

Niebuhr is right in criticizing Hegel for seeing history in too universal terms.[61] This had the effect of deifying the state.[62] C .S. Lewis wrote as Screwtape, one of Satan's high command:

> That invaluable man Rousseau first revealed it (hidden in the heart of this striving for liberty there was also a deep hatred of personal freedom). In his perfect democracy, you remember, only the state religion is permitted; slavery is restored, and the individual is told that he has really willed (though he didn't know it) whatever the government tells him to do. From that starting point, via Hegel (another indispensable propagandist on our side) we easily contrived both the Nazis and the Communist states.[63]

Brunner in a different way made something of the same sort of criticism. He pointed to the latent naturalism of the Hegelian philosophy of history. The dialectic of the historic process is combined with the naturalistic idea of development.[64]

Laski: The Marxian View of Law and the State

Just as Thomism has known a rejuvenation in our time in such affluent writers as Maritain and Gilson, so Marxism in the 1930s and early 1940s served as a creative starting point for many writers in this country and in England.[65] Reinhold Niebuhr's *Reflections at the End of an Era*, to mention one of his earlier books, dealt with the economic crisis from a Marxist-Christian point of view. It was only gradually that Niebuhr came to criticize Marxian self-righteousness for its lack of a transcendent perspective and its illusions about history and its necessary movement toward revolution. In any case, he had come to see that Marxian theory was a procrustean bed so far as fact and meeting were concerned by the time he wrote *The Nature and Destiny of Man* and had rid himself of his Marxian illusions and presuppositions.[66]

Laski felt that no one who studies the state operation seriously will fail to see bias in its operation. Since the Industrial Revolution, the state has been biased in favor of the owners of production as against those who have nothing but their labor to sell. This is only an example, however, for Laski was certain that this struggle has been going on since the earliest times. The extensive use of the machine has only intensified this struggle.

Written constitutions, Bills of Rights, the separation of powers, and fundamental law have all failed to persuade men that their objectives can be obtained without violence. This struggle is between various groups in a society. Doubtless the first struggle is in terms of the ideas that each group puts forward, but in time, if the conditions become hard enough, there is a struggle by the "have-nots" to seize the instruments of power and production "the haves" now own and control.

The reason this struggle is obscured, according to Laski, is that those who control an environment set the ideological pattern of thought. The group in power will hide a more acceptable ideology. Thus the Revolution of 1789 was fought in the name of universal principles of right, while actually the revolution was fought to free the middle-class owners of property from subjection to a state serving the privileged interest of the landed aristocracy.[67]

Laski states,

> The basic struggles, that is to say, are always struggles between economic classes to secure control of the sovereign power. An economic class may be defined as a group of people whose special place in the productive process is differentiated sharply from that of other groups. That place is defined by the system of economic relationships which the state maintains. The state puts at the service supreme coercive power which is its essence...[68]

According to Laski, the state is never neutral in political struggles of this kind. It does not stand over and above them judging impartially between them. Its very nature is coercive power to protect the system of rights and duties of one process of economic relations from invasions by another class.[69]

The essence of the state is power. It is the instrument of the class which happens to be dominant and in control of the means of production. This means that laws will be beneficial to the group in power and disadvantageous to other groups. Laski's argument can be illustrated from his description of Fascism. Fascism has entrusted unlimited political power to those who own and control the means of production. This class has built their authority in part upon an agreement with the armed forces of the state.[70]

One aspect of Marxian criticism which many feared would come to pass was the teaching that if change were to come, it would by necessity come by revolution. Laski taught, as Marx had before him, the inevitability of revolution as the midwife of change.[71] Having failed to wrest any power from the ruling class, the laboring class would resort to revolution to bring about change. However, this is not to deny that certain changes have been brought about in an expanding economic system. While expansion is taking place, men let their reason have greater sway than in static or contracting periods.

Laski saw religion as the unifier of the capitalistic class, but its allowing itself to be subordinated to the interests of the privileged along with the advent of science has deprived religion of the allegiance of men.[72] At best, he saw religion as naive in its hope that men would give up their state power, which by definition would be the destruction of the state power as it had existed.[73]

Niebuhr has rightly criticized Marxism for its rigidity in interpreting facts. Facts are seen from the presuppositions of Marxian theory and forced to fit that theory even though they obscure the true realities of the situation. Marxian theorists have not understood the pride or corruption of man; hence their self-righteous condemnation of others and at the same time their distortion of truth into propaganda for bolstering their criticism of others or their own positions of power in their world.[74]

Brunner has criticized this position by noting with Niebuhr that all facts cannot be fitted into its interpretation of history. He further criticized Marxism for being too fatalistic in its pattern to which all history must be fitted and the end toward which all history must move.[75]

ENDNOTES

1. Calvin, *The Institutes of the Christian Religion*, Vol. II, chapters I and XVIII.
2. Niebuhr, *The Nature and Destiny of Man*, Vol. I, p. 70.
3. Calvin, op. cit., Vols. II, IV, XX, XVIII.
4. Ibid., IV, XX, I.
5. Ibid., IV, XX, XI.
6. Ibid., IV, XX, IV, Rom. 13:4.
7. Ibid., IV, XX, VIII.
8. Ibid., IV, XX, XI.
9. Ibid., IV, XX, XIII.
10. Ibid., IV, XX, XV.
11. Matt. 5: 39, 40.

12. Ibid., 40.
13. Calvin, op. cit., Vols. IV, XX, XIX.
14. Acts. 5:28.
15. Op. cit., IV, XX, XXXIII.
16. Gettell, *History of Political Thought*, p. 172.
17. Ibid., p. 172.
18. Ibid., p. 173.
19. John Knox, *The History of rhe Reformation in Scotland* (one volume edition), p. 279.
20. Thomas Carlyle, *Heroes and Hero Worship*, p. 138.
21. Gettell, op. cit., p. 205.
22. Ibid., p. 206.
23. E. S. Bates, *American Faith*, p. 189.
24. Thomas Hobbes, *Leviathan*, introduction by Michael Oakeshott, p. viii.
25. Kant, *Theory and Practice*, p. 435.
26. Hobbes, *Leviathan*, p. 83.
27. Ibid., p. 84.
28. Ibid., p. 87.
29. Ibid., p. 89.
30. Ibid., p. xxxiii.
31. Ibid., p. 176.
32. Ibid., p. 174.
33. Ibid., p. 132.
34. Ibid., p. 240.
35. Brunner, *The Divine Imperative*, p. 576.
36. J. J. Rousseau, *The Social Contract*, introduction by Wilmore Kendell, p. vi.
37. *The Encyclopedia Britannica*, Vol. XIX, p. 585.
38. Rousseau, *The Social Contract*, p. 14.
39. Ibid., p. 3.
40. Ibid., p. 13.
41. Ibid., p. 7.

42. Ibid., p. 94. Rousseau saw reproduction as one good test of prosperity.
43. Ibid., p. 193.
44. Ibid., p. 123.
45. Ibid., p. 155.
46. Ibid., p. 153.
47. Ibid., p. 159.
48. Hegel, *The Philosophy of Law*, p. 447.
49. Ibid., p. 446.
50. Ibid., p. 447.
51. Hegel, *The Philosophy of History*, p. 417.
52. Ibid., p. 435.
53. Ibid., p. 412.
54. Hegel, *The Philosophy of Law*, p. 449.
55. Hegel, *The Philosophy of Law*, Friedrich, editor, p. 450.
56. Loc. cit., p. 455.
57. Loc. cit., p. 455.
58. Loc. cit.
59. Loc. cit., p. 465.
60. Loc. cit., p. 468.
61. Reinhold Niebuhr, *The Nature and Destiny of Man*, Vol. I, p. 80.
62. C .S. Lewis, "Screwtape Proposes a Toast," *Adventures of the Mind*, No. 42, *The Saturday Evening Post*, December 19, 1959, p. 88.
63. Ibid., p. 88.
64. Brunner, *The Divine Imperative*, p. 583.
65. C .S. Lewis, "Screwtape Proposes a Toast," *Adventures of the Mind* No. 42, *The Saturday Evening Post*, December 19, 1959, p. 88.
66. Niebuhr, *Nature and Destiny of Man*, Vol. I, p. 196.
67. Harold J. Laski, *The State in Theory and Practice*, p. 99.
68. Ibid., p. 100.
69. Loc. cit.
70. Ibid., p. 112.

71. Ibid., p. 119.
72. Ibid., p. 278.
73. Ibid., p. 252.
74. Niebuhr, *The Nature and Destiny of Man,* Vol. I, p. 197.
75. Brunner, *The Divine Imperative*, p. 427.

CHAPTER VI

Kant and Brunner on Justice

INTRODUCTION

A summary of the principles Kant and Brunner set forth should be given before dealing with particular problems. In subsequent chapters, the problem of justice in marriage, the problem of justice in the state, and the problem of international order will be dealt with. The last chapter will be an attempt to think through what the Christian idea of justice should be.

Both Kant and Brunner made serious attempts to arrive at the meaning of justice, or right, as Kant spoke of it. The confusion comes at this point in the translation of the German word *recht,* which can mean either law, right, or justice. In dealing with Kant, it seemed best to translate the *recht* as right, but it should be understood that Kant is speaking of that which is right or just.

Colleen Hutchins says, "Those people who are not governed by God will be ruled by tyrants."[1] In a broad sense both Kant and Brunner believed this, although with Kant God alone is the final guarantor of justice.

Kant's Concept of Right

Kant thought life would be easier if the laws of one's country would tell what is right. It is true that positive law tells what is right in a particular time and place. However, what must be done is to discover the criterion by which right and wrong may be ascertained. Kant was certain that pure reason will have to be the source of such judgments in order to lay a real foundation for actual positive legislation. Empirical laws may furnish guidance, but principles are the important thing. To proceed without principles would be like the wooden head in the fable of Phaedrus. The head was fine enough in appearance, but unfortunately it did not have any brains.[2]

The principle is not to be determined by the wish or the desire. Acts of will are important, but they must be free acts. They must harmonize with the freedom of others according to universal law.

Right, then, covers the whole of the conditions under which the voluntary actions of any one person can be harmonized with the voluntary actions of all other persons.

Although his thought on natural law is different from other eighteenth-century thinkers, Kant appealed to it, nevertheless.[3] Kant's natural law is the universal law of reason. He wrote:

> Every action is right which in itself, or on the maxim on which it proceeds, is such that it can co-exist along with the freedom of the will of each and all in action, according to universal law.[4]

A man then is wronged when someone interferes with his freedom. In the external consideration of the philosophy of law, *recht* this same man is not harmed if one only wishes to impinge his freedom but does nothing about it. However, in ethics such a feeling would be wrong, for ethics is concerned that each man make the fulfillment of right a maxim of his conduct.

Freedom which wrongs freedom is wrong. It is necessary when freedom is used to harm others that this use of freedom be restrained. Hence, the compulsion which restrains the wrong use of freedom is right.[5] This is, as it can clearly be seen, a logical argument for the freedom of all so long as the freedom of the neighbor is not impinged.

Right may be represented in a strict legal sense as the possibility of a universal reciprocal compulsion in harmony with the freedom of all according to universal law. The external is the sole measure of right according to the strict legal meaning. This is true of right in general. Strict legal rights are founded upon the consciousness of obligation of every individual according to law. Pure form should refer to this consciousness as a motive by which to determine the free act of the will. It must be grounded upon external compulsion brought upon him. The law of right amounts to a reciprocal compulsion necessarily in accordance with the freedom of every one under the principle of a universal freedom. This is to be an ideal, not an empirical statement. The principle is made known a priori by the reason. Individuals react upon one another under reciprocal compulsion within the framework of the principle of freedom. Kant does not want equity included in law, for, he thinks it is too inexact a science. It is impossible to know what equity will be in the particular situation.[6] The power of Kant's system lies in its determining of fundamental principles. These are to be regarded as an expression of the science of right.[7]

Kant divided the science of right into "General Division of the Duties of Right." In the first, he includes the three formulas of Ulpian. He developed them thus:

> 1. Honete Vive. Live rightly. Judicial rectitude or honor consists in maintaining one's worth as a man in relation to others. This duty may be rendered by the propositions: Do not make thyself a mere means for the use of others, but be to them likewise an end. This duty will be explained in the next formula as an obligation arising out of the right of humanity in our person.
>
> 2. Niminem Lede. Do wrong to no one. This formula may be rendered so as to mean: Do no wrong to anyone, even if thou shouldst be under the necessity, in observing this duty, to cease from all connection with others to avoid all society.
>
> 3. Suum cuique tribus. Assign to every one what is his own. This may be rendered: Enter, if wrong cannot be avoided, into society with others in which every one may have secured to him what is his own... Enter into a state in which every one can have what is his own secured against the action of every other.[8]

This system is divided into natural and positive right as a scientific system. Natural right rests upon rational principles a priori. Positive or statutory right is what proceeds from the will of the legislator. Rights can be looked at from another point of view. Each person possesses a legal foundation for his relations to every other person as a member of society. The system is divided into innate and acquired rights. Innate right is that which belongs to every one by nature, independent of all juridical acts of experience. Acquired rights are founded upon such juridical acts. Innate right may be called the "Internal Mine and Thine"; for external right must always be acquired.

Kant is convinced that there is only one inborn right and that is the right to freedom. Freedom is the independence of the compulsory will of all others. Equality, justice, and common action are also included in the principle of innate freedom. The latter means common action of the group so that others do not infringe their rights.

Previously, Kant had defined right from two points of view: the general division of the duties of right and the universal division of rights. Now, he makes a final classification. He calls this "The Methodical Division of the Science of Right." He says the division should be made into natural and civil rights. The natural rights are the private rights and the civil rights are the public rights. The whole of the principles of right fall under the two subdivisions of private and public right.[9]

Kant did not think he had set forth principles for all occasions of lawmaking, however, he did think he had set forth the principles that would guide in such an inquiry. He attempted to establish the formal principle by which the first principles of right could be tested. He thought that the principles of right would show a man how he is to live, in the family for instance.[10]

BRUNNER

Criticism of Kant

Brunner thought that Kant had the problem of getting from the sphere of obligation to that of existence. In other words, Kant's system logically holds together, but it is not able to be concrete. Yet, even so, Kant is quite down to earth in comparison with his younger contemporary Johann Fichte.[11] Kant's recognition of the evil nature of man has real roots in Christian teaching. According to Brunner, Kant's attempt to pass off the problem by blaming the empirical self does not go far enough, for there is still the problem of how the empirical self got that way.[12] Reason cannot be left untouched by the predicament. Yet, it is interesting that Brunner placed Kant with Luther and Kierkegaard as having understood the nature of evil better than many philosophers, Thomas Aquinas, to name an important one. St. Thomas, in contrast to Kant, saw good as made up of individual virtues. Luther and Kierkegaard saw sin as positional.[13]

Brunner pointed out that man is not really grasped as a person in Kant's philosophy, not as a real man. Reason always conceives of the other people in terms of their rationality, which is too impersonal. The real man, Brunner thought, is somewhere between the empirical, causally determined self and the intelligible self. Kant did not conceive of man who is both responsible and guilty.[14] Brunner pointed out that there are many different quotations in Kant in relation to God and ethics. However, there is at least one strong strain in Kant that held that God is reason:

> God is not being outside of me. He is merely a thought within me. God is the Reason which morally and practically posits itself as law... Thus God is not a substance which can be found outside me but merely a moral relation within me.[15]

There is little doubt that man in a state of original righteousness and justice could do the things that Kant has taught that man can do. The emphasis in the ethical works is "if you are commanded to be good, you can be."[16] This is Pelagian, and if man could do the command, there would be fewer problems for legal philosophy and for ethics, Niebuhr, on the other hand, accused Brunner of harboring the feeling "If you ought, you cannot."[17]

The Divine Command

One might think at first thought that the idea of God's sovereignty would be a rather nebulous basis for thinking about justice. At least, a person brought up on modern positivistic legal theory might think so. However, since Christianity has become strong enough to think seriously upon the subject, it has never been thought so by Christians. The divine command is the basis of our action. Brunner, in speaking of the divine commandment wrote that the commandments are not primarily the command, however they do help bear the command. For the commandments are primarily the law, and because the divine command is only through faith.[18]

The divine command gathers up into itself the meaning of all laws and gives them meaning and imperative. All the commands are gathered in the one command—to love our neighbor as ourselves.

The law referred to here is not positive law but rather the law of

God. So long as man lives on earth, he is bound to be a citizen of a state with its attempt at evenhanded justice. There is always an antithesis between justice and the law of love, for love makes a man a citizen of the heavenly kingdom. The antithesis and the bond both are always present.[19]

According to Brunner, love asks no questions about the nature of that which is to be loved. God loves the worthy but also the unworthy. No pagan knows this love. God is love according to the New Testament. This love judges not according to merits and incomprehensibly forgives sins.[20]

Justice is a totally different thing. Justice makes no free gift; it gives what is due and no more. It is realistic, sober, and rational. Justice is comprehensible to all.

Justice is rational, because it sees man in a rational system. It gives to each his due in a realistic and impersonal way. Justice is represented as blindfolded. It sees only the lawful right. Whoever a man is, he gets his due. Justice knows only intellectual value, the intelligible thing, the dignity of man. The just man recognizes the same dignity as he has himself, the quality as a person, the same general law of being.[21] This is quite different from love, as can be readily seen. Love loves a particular person in his uniqueness. Love loves him because he exists as another human being.[22]

Kant was afraid of love. He felt that passion and feeling kept one from duty. "Love, as an affection, cannot be commanded, but benevolence for duty's sake may." This is called "practical love." Love with feeling and affection or with sympathy he called "pathological love." Practical love was seated in the will.[23]

According to Kant, love that was sympathetic was heteronomous. Brunner held that love that was sympathetic was heteronomous. Brunner held that respect for persons is somewhat akin to the New Testament teaching on brotherly love.[24] Yet, the rational is too thoroughgoing in Kant at this point, and Brunner thought the lack was in reason's being unable to identify itself with the person to be loved in feeling. "The relation of reason to another person may be 'pure,' but it is always cold. On the other hand, love is both 'pure' and 'warm'."[25] Love sees the life of the other person as "my life." By faith the Christian sees the other person as "my life." By faith the Christian sees the other person as a fellow member in the Body of Christ. If one member suffers, all the members suffer. God does not respect us; he loves us.[26]

However, justice is for Brunner a different order of creation. Justice does not make use of this love; indeed it does not need to, since it is never concerned with human beings as such but with human beings in relationship. Justice belongs to the world of systems and not to the world of persons. Since persons are higher than systems, systems are made for the persons. Love transcends justice. In its own way, justice is supreme. Within the system as such nothing is higher than justice, however, love is higher in a deeper sense, since it is concerned with persons and not just systems.

The Christian does not cease to love in the realm of systems. Rather, he gives effect to his love by being just. He changes his love into the coin of justice, since that is the legal tender of systems.[27] Niebuhr has criticized this position of Brunner. Niebuhr's emphasis has been that love is the highest possibility of man in his relationship to man. It is the highest possibility in his social nature as well. Christianity must insist on the relevance of the ideal to all moral experience of mankind on every conceivable level of life. The ideal of love is involved in every moral aspiration and achievement.[28]

Justice is not enough even in the realm of systems for Niebuhr. Love is thus the end term of any system of morals. It is the moral requirement in which all schemes of justice are fulfilled and negated. They are fulfilled because the obligation of life to life is more fully met in love than is possible in any scheme of equity and justice. They are negated because love makes an end of the nicely calculated less and more of structures of justice. It does not carefully arbitrate between the needs of the self and of the other, since it meets the needs of the other without concern for the self.[29]

Another aspect of this problem of love Niebuhr saw in the possibilities of forgiveness in the Christian understanding of love. The Marxian has his self-righteousness precisely because he does not understand the depth of human sins, and this means his own self as well as others. Hence, he sees no need for forgiveness or for the mitigating certainy of a love that carries with it forgiveness. Yet, it is this possibility of love that holds out the promise of mitigation in the conflicts of life.[30]

In some of his works Niebuhr has spoken of the appeal to justice as second-rate Christianity. However, what he meant was that justice is an approximation of human brotherhood under the approximation of sin. He has made a great deal of justice as a balance of power.[31]

At the same time, Niebuhr has recognized that a higher justice always means a more equal justice. Special privilege may be frowned upon more severely by those who want it than those who have it, but those who have it are always uneasy in their conscience about it.[32]

Justice

Justice is indispensable in the world of systems in Brunner's thinking. It is always inferior compared with love. In the realm of institutions, love which is not justice is sentimentality. In this case, such feeling for feeling's sake is a poison. It is the solvent which destroys all just institutions.

The more closely institutions approach the personal sphere, the smaller the number of human beings it embraces, and the less things in it predominated over persons the greater the chance for love to make its influence felt. On the other hand, the state is the most impersonal of human institutions because the number of persons is greater than other institutions, and there are a greater number of other institutions ruled by it.[33]

On the other hand, love has predominance in marriage; yet in marriage there is is always the element of justice, for the duty the husband owes to the wife is not the same as the wife owes to the husband. Even the most perfect marriage is an institution. Between marriage and the state there are manifold institutions of social life, which according as persons or things predominate in their purpose, are ruled more by justice or by love. Because man is man, he is a member of an institution. However, there is still room for love even in the most impersonal of institutions.[34]

Justice is the precondition of love; love must never neglect justice. For it becomes something less than love in so doing. Love ought to do more, never less than justice demands. It must fulfill the impartial law of justice and then go beyond justice. Only love can be perfectly just. Brunner gave the analogy of the glass of water, full and running over, to express the relation between love and justice. Love can fulfill justice, but it can never itself be fulfilled. Love by definition has to be without measure or calculation. This kind of love is only fulfilled in God.[35]

Brunner on Justice and the Law of Nature

Brunner pointed to three ways of looking at the law of nature. 1. The objective and collective law of nature of the pre-Christian world. 2. The subjective and individualistic law of nature of modern times.

3. The Christian law of nature. He saw the pre-Christian objective type as pointing to a nature which was rational. This rational nature ordered the cosmos. This reason pervading the cosmos is what all justice is based on.

The modern view has seen nature as almost equivalent to human reason. This makes the law of nature too individualistic.

The Christian view of the law of nature sees nature as under the control of divine reason and is ruled by divine reason. Nature is the divine creative ordinance of God—the God who made himself and his will known in Jesus Christ.[36]

In all these views, there is one common thing, a justice which transcends human caprice and convention. They all seek some standard of judging the state and its laws. The positive law is to give effect to the law of nature.

All three views contain not only a formal idea of justice, but they also contain certain fundamental standards of an actual just order. The formal idea means that every judge and legislator must try to do justice according to certain basic principles.

As has been noted, the law of nature means that there are certain principles that are basic and to which appeal can be made for justice. The prime example is the claim for the primal and basic rights of man, for there are certain rights which are inherently just and inalienable. These rights are each man's due.[37] Opponents of the law of nature are really criticizing Grotius's view and other philosophers of the Age of Reason. The critics usually ignore the classical, Stoic, and Christian views. For at all times what has been meant by the law of nature is a moral principle of justice which subjects and regulates the natural instincts of man, whether the regulation be one of the instinct, or power, gain, or of sex. The doctrine of the law of nature in Western tradition has always been antinaturalistic. The concept of "nature" upon which it has been based has always been theological and moral. The concept underlying this principle has nothing in common with what today is known as the law of nature. There is a general tendency to reject the idea today because of what has been taking place in the last three centuries.[38]

Jurists have felt the need to reject the individualistic conception. However, having done this, they were left with nothing but positive law. This rejection of natural law prepared the way for the totalitarian state from which there could be no appeal, because it was the source of its own law and allowed no questions or appeal to anything except itself.[39]

If there is no acknowledgment of the Creator and his order of creation, and its concomitant principle to each his due, there can be no permanent order of justice. The rights of man must be recognized as the rights God has given.[40]

The difference between Protestant and Catholic thinkers in their teaching on the law of nature corresponds to their difference in the assessment of rational knowledge. The Reformers stressed the fact that sin has obscured the capacity of human reason even in the spheres which are accessible to human knowledge. Yet, they recognized that the justice man has comes from his deduction of justice based on the knowledge of the orders of creation.

There are two important emphases in Brunner's thought. It could be said that there are two aspects of justice. 1. That which is just in itself. It is based on the divinely created nature of man and presupposes it. 2. The relative justice in reference to a reality which has fallen away from creation.[41] The absolute justice would not be the best justice in the fallen world, for it would have an effect contrary to the effect sought. Every positive system of justice has to be a compromise between the truly just and what is possible. The possible has to take into consideration the demand for justice and the given circumstances. "The optimum of the relatively just lies between over readiness to adapt to reality and accessible right in maintaining the abstract idea of absolute justice."[42]

Niebuhr criticized the theory of natural law by pointing to the tendency of every age to absolutize its own ideals. The Thomistic definitions of justice were filled with specific details of the feudal political order. When the bourgeois of the eighteenth century came into power they invented new natural law theories and invested them with bourgeois, rather than feudal aristocratic content. According to Niebuhr, the natural law theory of each is used to justify the class power in any particular age. In short, it is not possible to state a universally valid concept of justice from any particular sociological locus in history. Nor is it possible to avoid either making the effort or making the pretenses of universality which human finiteness does not justify.[43]

Brunner on Equality

Kant taught that there is an innate equality that belongs to every man. This right consists in man's right to be independent of being bound by others to anything more than that which may reciprocally bind them. There is an inborn quality that every man ought to be his own master.[44]

In practice, Kant limited the right of men to certain positions. Servants and those in menial positions had their political rights abridged. Kant did not mean this to do away with the innate dignity and equality in men.[45]

Brunner's criticism of Kant is that man is valued in his system for his reason rather than his personhood. The point of the criticism is that reason is impersonal and makes it hard to treat the other person any other way. Rather, Brunner pointed out, man in Christian thought is personal because of his being made in the image of God. Man derives his personhood from God. This makes him addressable by God.[46]

According to Brunner, law establishes a merely formal equality. It does not tell us what may be due each; it merely says that whatsoever may be due the individual shall be created according to law. To each his due is the Christian principle. This is different than to each the same which is the legal category for each class as normally conceived. Yet, justice is related to equality. Brunner is not depreciating law which implies equalization of as many as fall within its classification. He recognized that law gives security by establishing a sameness for tomorrow as well as for yesterday. He is trying to get back of the justice of human codes, to get at the justice to which all human law looks and which enables us to say, "This law is unjust."[47]

Brunner affirmed both equality and inequality. His emphasis on the inequalities is somewhat repugnant to modern man who is used to emphasizing equality. Yet, it is necessary to look at the inequalities, however little the idea appeals to modern presuppositions and prejudices.

Human beings are never equal really.[48] They can be treated as equals only in so far as the inequalities are regarded as not as important as the equalities. A case in point is not treating less-gifted and brilliant children the same. The problem boils down to which is considered the most important, the equalities or the inequalities.[49]

The Stoic taught equality, Brunner noted, but this equality is an abstract equality and never had the force that the Gospel came to have. There was a blending of the Stoic and Christian views into the doctrine of the equal dignity of all human beings.[50]

The Stoics view had been that an impersonal reason or *nous* pervades all things, and all human beings substantially participate in this reason. From this men derive their dignity. The Christian view is unconditionally personal. The Christian God creates man and predestinates him for communion and love. Man's dignity comes not from his humanity derived from a universal reason, but from his addressability. Individual personality is determined by the will of God and is as important as the general dignity of humanity. Every human person has his dignity which comes from his predestination to personal being as is the case of every other human being. God loves each man individually. Man's inequality springs from the same root as his equality.

Brunner thought the Biblical view of the sexes differed from the Stoic view. The Stoic view held the differences between men and women were unimportant, but the Bible considers them important. The Bible invests the differences with consummate dignity, the dignity of creation. Yet, human beings in Christian thought, Brunner pointed out, are also equal. They have the same dignity and equality of responsibility to God. Each has the right to be recognized as a person. Christianity sees men as a fellowship of persons in love and responsibility. Christianity puts equality and equal rights in a place of primary importance in its thinking on justice, while inequality still is very important and inescapable.[51]

Niebuhr pointed out that the ones who have privilege are the ones who like to point out the need for inequalities, while those who are victims of inequality see the hypocrisy in this approach. According to him, a higher justice always means a more equal justice. Brunner may try to dismiss the need for equality as Stoic egalitarianism and call it presumption and desire to tell the Creator what he ought to have done at creation, but that would be to miss the point that children have the natural desire to be treated alike, and they are unperverted by Stoic rationalism.[52]

Summary

For Kant right is known by the formulations of reason according to universal law. One of the maxims of reason is the maxim of the freedom of each so long as this freedom does not hinder the neighbor in his freedom. Right may be represented as the possibility of a universal reciprocal compulsion to guarantee the freedom of all and in harmony with the freedom of all according to universal law.

There is, according to Kant, only one inborn right and that is the right to freedom. Freedom is the independence of the compulsory will of all other wills. Equality, justice, and common action are included in the principle of innate freedom.

According to Brunner, Kant put the emphasis on the universal principle set up by reason when it should have been put on divine command to really secure justice. This is so, for men do justice because it is God's command. This means that love furnishes the final motivation. Although love is not the same as justice for Brunner, it still furnishes the final motivation, for it guarantees justice and more. Hence, the emphasis for justice should not be placed primarily on governmental theory in the consideration of justice, but on God's command and man's ability to obey.

Brunner viewed justice as a different order from love. Justice is an order of creation set up to give each man his due. It is rational and impersonal. Love is God's agape for man. On the human level, it is personal concern for other persons without regard for their own worthiness. It asks no questions but gives because God loves both the worthy and the unworthy.

The Christian does not love in the realm of systems. He gives effect to his love by being just. He changes his love into the coin of justice, since that is the legal tender of systems.

Kant has emphasized the innate equality that belongs to every man. Brunner considers this an abstract principle emphasizing the likeness of men rather than their unlikeness. Men and women are different in their function in the area of sex, for instance, according to God's order of creation. Again, men are different in ability. It would not be equity to treat men and women the same in all cases, nor would it be equity to treat people the same without consideration of their talents and abilities. However, there is a primal likeness in that all men are equally responsible before God and equally addressable by God.

Niebuhr questioned the division of justice and love as set up in Brunner's thought. He believed that even in the realm of systems love should be a mitigation and ideal. It is doubtful that he makes too much of an improvement, however, for justice admittedly becomes second-rate love.

In the consideration of equality and inequality, Niebuhr found Brunner's weak point, although this does not mean that Brunner is wrong. It means only that Brunner emphasized too strongly the Stoic element in equality. Having examined past history, Niebuhr was quite correct to emphasize the misuse of the fact of inequality. It is almost always the well-off who are glad to emphasize the inequalities of life as being true to the way men are built. The less well-off, Niebuhr learned from Marx, are inclined to see the hypocrisy of the claim as a mask for privilege.

ENDNOTES

1. Colleen Hutchins in *Faith Made Them Champions*, edited by Norman Vincent Peale, p. 87.
2. Kant, *The Philosophy of Law*, p. 44.
3. Kant, *Eternal Peace*, p. 446.
4. Kant, *The Philosophy of Law*, p. 45. The situation where Kant appealed to natural law was against ships being robbed along the Barbary Coast and Bedouine robbing travelers in the desert. He said it was contrary to natural law. National pride prompts the observation that it was the warships of the young United States which put an end to the piracy along the Barbary Coast.
5. Ibid., p. 47.
6. Ibid., pp. 49-50.
7. Cairns, *Legal Philosophy from Plato to Hegel*, p. 409.
8. Kant, *The Philosophy of Law*, pp. 54-55.
9. Ibid., pp. 57-58.
10. Cairns, *Legal Philosophy from Plato to Hegel*, p. 413.
11. Brunner, *The Divine Imperative*, p. 39.
12. Ibid., p. 590.
13. Ibid., p. 605.
14. Ibid., p. 702.
15. Ibid., quoted Op. Post. p. 786.
16. Kant, *Religion Within the Limits of Reason*, p. 398.
17. Niebuhr, *Christian Realism and Political Problems*, p. 151.
18. Brunner, *The Divine Imperative*, p. 112.
19. Brunner, *Justice and the Social Order*, p. 114.
20. Ibid., p. 114.

21. Ibid., p. 116. David Roberts has this to say that goes along with Brunner at this point. It also supports the thesis of this work that the problem of justice is the problem of man and his place in the God-created order. Roberts writes: "Democracy stands or falls on the attitude toward the person. The question is not merely whether he is free, in a technical sense, to vote, to work, to speak and to worship. The question is also whether he is looked upon as a responsible spiritual being instead of a cog in a social machine." *What the Christian Hopes for in Society*, edited by Wayne H. Cowan, Roberts' essay, "The Christian Gospel," p. 75.
22. Brunner, *Justice and the Social Order*, p. 116.
23. Kant, *Metaphysics of Morals*, Abbot, Editor, p. 16.
24. Brunner, *Justice and the Social Order*, p. 117.
25. Brunner, *The Divine Imperative*, p. 322.
26. Ibid., p. 322.
27. Op. cit., p. 116.
28. Niebuhr, *An Interpretation of Christian Ethics*, pp. 104-105.
29. Niebuhr, *The Nature and Destiny of Man*, Vol. I, p. 295.
30. Niebuhr, *Love and Justice*, W. D. Robinson, editor, p. 46.
31. Niebuhr, *An Interpretation of Christian Ethics*, p. 191.
32. Niebuhr, *The Nature and Destiny of Man*, Vol. I, pp. 254-255.
33. Brunner, *Justice and the Social Order*, p. 116.
34. Ibid., p. 117.
35. Ibid., p. 118.
36. Ibid., p. 81.
37. Ibid., p. 113.
38. Ibid., p. 82.
39. Ibid., p. 83.
40. Ibid., p. 84. John Bennett has emphasized the fact of the Lordship of God. From this he infers that the structure of life is favorable to the continuation of his creative work. Because of God's Lordship men live under "common grace" in society. *What the Christian Hopes for in Society*, editor, Wayne H. Cowan. John Bennett's Essay, "What Can We Hope for in Society?" p. 29.
41. Brunner, *Justice and the Social Order*, p. 95.

42. Ibid., p. 95.
43. Niebuhr, *Love and Justice*, the essay "Christian Faith and Natural Law, p. 49.
44. Kant, *The Philosophy of Law*, p. 56.
45. Ibid., p. 168.
46. Brunner, *The Divine Imperative*, p. 584.
47. Brunner, *Justice and the Social Order*, p. 27.
48. Trueblood sees men as created equal, but he also sees their inequalities, mental, physical, and even spiritual. Democracy certainly does not mean that every man's opinion is equally valid. He wrote, "If democracy means that one man's opinion is just as valid as another's, democracy is obviously doomed." Trueblood, *Declaration of Freedom*, p. 73. In another place he wrote, All men are equal because all men are different from the rest of creation. Men differ from one another in degree, but they differ from all other creatures in kind." Ibid, p. 75.
49. Ibid., p. 33.
50. Ibid., p. 38.
51. Ibid., p. 45.
52. Niebuhr, *The Nature and Destiny of Man*,Vol. II, p. 256.

CHAPTER VII

Kant and Brunner on Family

KANT

Introduction

Kant set up a rational jurisprudence which is complete so far as the main principles are concerned. He means his legal theory to be a part of his ethics. Basic to his thought is that in the inner world of the moral self man is in the presence of the "ought." By virtue of his reason man can attain knowledge of human contact and from the legislative principles all positive law can be deduced. Kant held that ethics makes the principle the norm for personal conduct, whereas law deals with external actions. Ethics imposes the obligation of the "ought"; law imposes obligation but there is the element of compulsion which limits freedom. While marriage comes under the section on "Private Right: The System of Those Laws Which Require No External Promulgation," certainly Kant meant that the rights and duties in the area of domestic relations were to be as thoroughly legal as those in the section entitled "Public Right."[1]

Personal right of a real kind is one of the categories of mine and thine. It concerns the right to possession of the external object as a thing and to the use of it as a person. This sounds like a violation of treating each person as an end and never a means, but apparently Kant meant the impersonalism to be negated by the mutuality of the relationship, for he used the phrase "intercommunity of the sexes." This relationship may be in the realm of animal nature or according to law. The latter is called marriage. He defined marriage as "the union of two persons of different sex for life-long reciprocal possession of their sexual faculties."[2] The marriage has as its end the producing and the educating of children. However, there is the erotic urge as well; otherwise the marriage would dissolve when there were no longer any children.

The Meaning of Marriage

Marriage is for the enjoyment in the reciprocal use of the sexual endowments, yet the contract of marriage is not a matter merely of arbitrary will but is necessary by the law of humanity. This dictation of the necessity to marry so as to enjoy the benefits of marriage is in accordance with the juridical laws of pure reason.[3] Kant admitted that the human individual (according to the rational right of marriage) makes himself a "res" which is contrary to the right of humanity, in his own person. This is alleviated by the reciprocity of the relationship. However, the other also becomes a "res."

This relationship is real in kind. The marriage gives the other title to the one married so that if one person runs away or enters into a relationship with another, the wronged party may have the party doing the wrong brought back. Kant added "as if the other were a thing."[4]

The relationship of the married people to each other is one of equality; this means mutual possession of their persons and their goods. This state calls for monogamy; for in polygamy the person who is given away gains only a part of the other person and makes the one given become a mere "res." It would appear that for a true marriage there has to be full mutual control of the person. This applies to the goods also, unless by special contract another agreement is reached.

Concubinage is a hiring of the other person for fornication. This is an illegal relationship and the person making the contract cannot be held to it. This would be enforcing the surrender of the one person to the arbitrary will of another.[5]

Kant's thought here would be pretty much the same as common law:

> Agreements which threaten the security of a family are not recognized and encouraged by the state and are illegal as against public policy. The institution of marriage is in this class. Accordingly agreements between married people for future separation, contracts not to marry, or marriage brokerage contracts are void as tending to injure the marital relation.[6]

It is certain as a matter of public policy that contracts that are immoral are illegal and not enforceable as common law.[7]

Kant did not think that marriages which establish the supremacy of the one party over the other are valid, because this could mar the equality of marriage. But the fact that the husband is the head of the house does not discount this ruling, for he is presumed to have greater faculties and the common interest of the household requires it. Presumably if it could be shown that if the wife had superior faculties the situation would be reversed.[8]

A marriage can be completed only by sexual intercourse. Contracts of marriage where one is permitted to abstain from conjugal cohabitation or where one party is incapacitated for it are dissolved at the will of either party. However, if the incapacity came after marriage, the marriage is not dissolved, for this is one of the contingencies of life.[9]

Parents and Children

Man has a duty toward himself, a duty toward humanity in his own person, which gives him the right to acquire a woman to be his wife. In like manner, the woman has the right to acquire a husband. From this proceeds conjugal relations and procreation. There then follows the duty of preserving and rearing children as products of this union. Children have a congenital right to be reared with care by their parents until they are capable of maintaining themselves. This proceeds from the law of reason without any juridical act being required. This is the principle, but, of course, there would be law or "prescription," to use Kant's language, to enforce the law.[10] Perhaps the nearest to this concept in American law would again be public policy. All the states have laws to enforce parental care, even as Kant suggested there should be.

The reason for the parents' responsibility, according to Kant, is that they bring the child into the world without the child's consent and the child becomes a person with freedom and rights. The child cannot be regarded merely as a thing of their own making, for a being so endowed cannot be so regarded. Nor can they destroy it, for they have placed a new being in the world whom they cannot treat with indifference, since God has created the child a free human being.

The parent has the right and the responsibility to take care of the child's physical needs and to educate and train him so that when he reaches maturity he will be able to make a living in the world. The parent is to concern himself with more than just the physical well-being of the child; he is to train the child morally and culturally. If the parent does not do this training, he is to be held guilty of neglect. Such training is to continue until the child is able to support himself and thus be emancipated. The parent then renounces the right to command the child. The parent cannot demand payment for what he has spent on the child any more than his own parents had the right to demand payment from him. The only appeal to the child, then, will be on the ground of obligation, of gratitude as a duty and a virtue.[11]

Although Kant would not have let himself be affected by it, it is possible that he knew the English common law on parent-child relations. It is well known that Kant admired the English form of government. Even if he did know the English law at this point, it would not have affected him unless he considered the principle involved to be one arrived at by reason.[12]

It is interesting, nevertheless, to find the common law ruling the same: The parent actually furnishing the child with necessary support and maintenance is denied any right to charge the child with the necessaries so furnished.[13] It should be pointed out that "necessaries" of common law were considered in relation to the wealth and the cultural status of the parents, which is also what Kant is saying.

According to Kant, the fact of personality in the child keeps the parent from ever regarding him as property. The right of the parent is the right of protection. The right, moreover, is inalienable; it is a personal right which may allow the child to be returned if he runs away.[14]

There was a principle of the common law which Kant did not consider. It is not possible to know what he would have thought of it. This law allowed the parents to have the child's earnings until the child was twenty-one. This is such a settled right in the common law that the parent may assign the child's wages to a third party.[15]

Kant wrote that, as soon as the child reaches the age of emancipation, the child is free to set up his own household without any question. However, if he continues in the household of his parents there is a new relation of master and servant. This relationship is governed by different rules. The condition may not be regulated by contract.[16]

Master and Servant

The master owns the servant who works for him as if by real right; for if he runs away he may be brought back under the master's will. The master is not entitled to conduct himself toward the servant as if he owned him. The servant is, however, subject to the master through contract, and this implies certain definite restrictions. The restrictions are that the servant cannot contract to give up his right to be a free person, nor can the master force the servant to give up his freedom. The reason Kant thought this could not be done is that he considered it to be a contradiction. Men have innate freedom and they cannot give it up.[17]

The contract, according to Kant, must carry implicitly the further restriction that the master can never abuse his servant. The master is not the sole judge of right. The servant has a voice also. A servant can never be permitted to become a serf, nor can a contract of this nature be for life. Rather a definite period should be specified. At the end of this time there may be a termination of the contract or a renewal at the will of the parties.[18]

It is interesting that Kant did not give as much attention to the problem of master and servant as was given in the common law.[19] The transfer was made in common law to interpret the employee as the servant. The rules were definitely slanted in favor of the master, the employer, and almost every case in the courts was rendered in favor of the employer. This was particularly harsh on labor in accident cases, where the so-called fellow servant rule was in effect. This meant that if an injury was caused by a fellow servant, the employer was released from payment for injury. With the growth of labor unions, labor exerted a stronger voice in legislation. Laws friendly to labor were passed, and the classification became "employer and employee" instead of "master and servant." Workmen's compensation laws have taken care of most of the labor injury cases where the injury took place on the job.[20]

Brunner on Marriage

The Point of Disagreement Between Brunner and Kant

In Brunner's thinking, Kant's approach to the problem of marriage demonstrated to a high degree the fault with the rationalistic approach. He pointed to Kant's teaching on marriage as the mutual lease of the sexual organs of the wife and husband as demonstrating to the full this impersonalism.[21]

The real reasons Kant has this problem with marriage is that his whole ethics is impersonal. His ethics is impersonal because the self-legislating reason sets up law which interposes itself between husband and wife, neighbor and neighbor. With this "something" between them a direct relation is impossible. The reason sets up the categorical imperative which renounces all experience in its choice of ends, but in renouncing all relation with experience it remains abstract and impersonal. The law is an abstract law of obligation. It does not put one in touch with the divine or the human "Thou," but with an abstract principle "reason." The final motive is really self-respect. Responsibility, whether it be to God, to the wife, or to the neighbor is distorted into a legalistic responsibility to the self. There is no relation to the "Thou" but to the "I."[22] While Kant admits the erotic, he is afraid of love. Really, whatever goes beyond the bounds of rational self-respect is for him erroneous.

The Argument for Monogamy

Brunner has a different basis for holding that monogamy should be practiced. Kant had held that the reason for monogamy was equality and the mutual possession of the married people's persons and their goods. Polygamy allows for a gaining of only a part of the other person and so makes him a "res." Brunner placed his argument in the order of nature.

According to Brunner, the principle of monogamy may be defined as that in which the husband and wife live together in exclusive life-long relationship. This relationship was taken for granted in the past once the couple were married. However, this can no longer be assumed in the present economic and industrial order. The disintegration of the monogamous relationship presents the Christian ethic with one of the most serious and difficult problems with which it has to deal. So serious is this problem that Brunner says that even the question of economic and political justice are of secondary importance in comparison. Here the problem is human existence and all ethical questions come together at one point.[23]

When the problem is seriously studied, the irreplaceable value of the family for procreation and for spiritual and moral education of children is perceived. The values of monogamy become apparent when the education and growth of children is so considered, for neither promiscuity, polygamy, nor polyandry give unity or permanence to the family.

The rationalist theory bases its argument for monogamy on procreation as the end of marriage. The subjective emphasis is on the erotic together with the cult of romance and love. The Christian faith bases its demand for monogamy on something which is beyond this antithesis. The subjective and the objective are united and based on something higher, that is, on the divine order of creation. It is true that every natural order of creation has been obscured by the presence of sin, and thus ignored, but God's order cannot be eliminated. This order is something of which even the "natural man" is somehow aware, even if it be not known as it really is. The true meaning is disclosed in faith.[24]

The meaning of the divine order of creation in marriage is this. It is life in community of two persons of different sexes, a community which is complete, based upon the natural foundation of sex love, but only fulfilled in the feeling that by divine appointment they belong to each other. It is through this created distinctiveness that the Creator maintains the human race. Marriage is, in a special sense, proof of the divine wisdom of the Creator, since in marriage the natural is directed in such a way that it leads both to the personal character of intimate life in community and to the universal purpose of the human species. Marriage, Brunner liked to emphasize, only realizes its true meaning in ever renewed responsible action. Marriage is the school of community created by God. In this school man can learn that he cannot live as an individual, but only as he is bound up with the other, and that each man has received his own life from such a connection between two persons.[25]

In this reaction against so-called romantic love which is really Hollywood sentimentality, Brunner emphasized that the relation between man and wife is one of fidelity. The Creator has called to the love relationship the two who are to live in this oneness. This relationship of fidelity means more than the "making use" of the other, even though this "use" may be mutual and willed by both sides.

This statement obviously refers critically to Kant as has been noted above. Brunner is certainly right in saying that the Kantian approach to sex is "subpersonal" and does not allow for a real identification with the other person. Fidelity has the responsibility which recognizes that one is bound to the other person. It is God's pedagogy which teaches man to understand the meaning of the personal though the experience of laws as an existence in community.[26]

Marriage As It Really Is

When one looks at marriage from the standpoint of the divine ordinance of creation, the idea of marriage is never the same as the reality, anymore than the real human being corresponds to the idea of man as the image of God. Just as there are only sinful human beings, so there are only sinful marriages, that is, marriages which at the same time amount to adultery. There is always the adultery of desire. This is the concupiscence of the soul which sees attractions of the opposite sex as both beauty and the object of desire. This desire, which is refined adultery, is not a legal category but an ethical one. Although this desire is ethically condemned, the lustful look can never be made the object of legal prosecution.[27]

Strangely enough, Kant could speak of the evil principle, or the evil element in man, when he is dealing with government.[28] But he nowhere touched upon the problem in marriage and the family. The whole approach is rational and impersonal. There is a sense in which one can speak of man's self-estrangement so that in the most intimate act of life, sexual intercourse, there is a sense of estrangement, but Kant knew nothing of this. He rather speaks of the opposite party as a "res."[29] Brunner sought the true relation between man and wife in the "I" of the one person confronting the "Thou" of the other person.[30] It is true that Brunner allows that lust without love can make the other partner a thing, but in the God relationship the other person is a person to be loved with *agape* and with *eros*. Where there is the *agape* the *eros* is redeemed and commanded *eros*.[31]

The divine command may show men their true selves in their sinfulness; however, the legal category of obedience to the Seventh Commandment can be obeyed in its legal connotations. There is the will of God which is higher than the Old Testament understanding. Jesus reinterpreted the Old Testament to condemn the desire held in thought. This understanding is ethical. God established the order of creation that men might be able in the order of law and the state have a knowledge of justice.

Justice in Marriage

So far what has been said about Brunner on marriage has been more in the subjective sphere, the experiential sphere of ethics. It is in order now to deal with the theoretical problem of justice as such in marriage. The adultery of desire is sinful, but only justice can measure the actual faithfulness. Love is necessary in marriage and is the stuff of which marriage should be made; however, the measure in the realm of what is due the partner and the children is justice.

There has been over the last two centuries a popular notion that the bond of love (*eros*) is the only thing that matters. While to an important extent this is true, this particular outlook has had some unfortunate results. Marriage often has been seen only in the form of a free contract, which, freely concluded, may be just as freely abolished or dissolved. The Christian view of "what God has joined let no man put asunder" is not considered seriously in its true import.[32] Marriage is an order of creation. Man is so made by God that his nature can have its true fulfillment only in a union with one woman, which union is continuous for a whole lifetime. The personalities of all members of the family can have their full development only in this type of union. Justice appears in marriage in the form of an indissoluble and strictly exclusive monogamy. In the order of creation there is the factor of personal equality and dignity not achievable outside the recognition of this order.[33]

In the order of creation there is the further factor of likeness of dignity united with the unlikeness of function. In the marriage relationship this is fully made apparent. The husband and wife have a full equality of worth. To seek to express that equality in all the relationships of marriage is to seek to fulfill the law of justice in marriage. The next step expresses the unlikeness of function. Each gives to the other his due, but what the husband owes to the wife is not the same as what the wife owes to the husband. In sex this is seen as the husband not belonging to himself but to the wife and the wife not to herself but to the husband. The husband has the right to his wife and she to her husband. The husband and wife render due benevolence to each other. Where the marriage is good each will render this due without the intervention of an objective imperative of justice. According to Brunner, this obligation means keeping himself only for the other partner and not allowing the relationship to be diverted by a third party. Justice appears in marriage as the prohibition of adultery in any form.

There is equality with a difference in function. This equality of dignity does not do away with a certain difference in kind and function. The equality of dignity does not do away with a certain hierarchy of organization. "The husband is head of the wife."[34] This is, in Brunner's thought, as much an order of creation as the principle of monogamy. It makes for the "natural" way God planned it. He noted that the rationalists, among whom he doubtless included Kant, do not see this difference of function and hierarchy of relationship. The order of creation is a patriarchate, not a matriarchate. This cannot in true Christianity degenerate into tyranny, because there is the Biblical stipulation of mutual obligation in which the equality of personal dignity finds expression.[35]

Marriage is meant to be indissoluble in the order of creation. However, due to the hardness of men's hearts Brunner allows divorce, though he reduces the possibility to the minimum required by the circumstances. A legal system has to concern itself with adultery if it is to maintain a strict order of divorce.

The state has to be concerned with the family and its stability. The beginning of national anarchy starts with anarchy in family relationships. The state in which divorce and adultery are the order of the day is certainly in the throes of moral decay.[36]

The Family

The foundation of real marriage is the monogamous marriage. The child gives to this permanent relationship much of its real meaning. Divorce is especially a catastrophe for the children, just as adultery is a confusion and a breaking up of the secure world of the adult. There must be the one father and one mother in love giving meaning to the child. Aside from this, the child finds it hard to find meaning and security. Sexual differentiation in creation has no other meaning. It is only in respect to the child that we can understand the fact that we are created different sexually. The religious view at this point tallies with biology. The sexual apparatus serves procreation.[37]

There is in the family a justice answering to the order of creation. The importance of the child is imparted by the order of creation. This makes the parents responsible to use their sexual functions, not for selfishness; in the words of Scripture, "Be fruitful and multiply."[38] Marriages which are deliberately childless are wrong; where unavoidable, they are unfortunate.

The relation of the child to the parents is an area where each has equal dignity, but with a difference. The primal rights of the child are equal to the parents. The child has a sacred right against the parents to be looked after and loved by the parents. If this right is neglected in certain cases the community has the duty to step in for the protection of the child. The iniquity of divorce can be deduced from the right of the child against the father and mother. The child is wronged if he loses either father or mother by divorce. The child is wronged because he does not have the love and protection of the parents, which is his due. If human laws do not work to protect the child, the laws so pertaining are unjust. The protection that is found in modern law is the direct fruit of Christianity.[39]

The emancipation of the child and the adolescent from the family union is not the fruit of Christianity, but of individualism. While Christianity teaches the dignity of the child, it at the same time teaches the difference in function between the different members of the family. All members belong to each other, the parents to the child and the child to the parents, just as the husband belongs to the wife and the wife to the husband. The manner of belonging is not the same. This manner of belonging creates an otherness, which is determined by the order of creation. Without any prejudice to the equal dignity of each member of the family, there is an unequivocal hierarchy. The father is the head of the family. The place of each member is determined by his function. The hierarchal order is father, mother, children. Brunner claimed this corresponds to natural feeling. Of course, the child goes on his own when he is of age. A just civil law gives expression to this order of creation without infringing the rights of the child as a person. The child has a right to the authority of the parent and misses something if he does not receive it.[40]

Each person has his rights and there is no real love until the demands of justice are met. A husband who does not give his wife justice in his treatment of her would not really be able to show love. A husband could not beat his wife each day and still show her proper love, for she has the right to be treated as an equal.

In this country under the old common law a married woman had no right to property. As soon as she was married, all her property came under the control of the husband. If he claimed it during his lifetime, he could treat it as his own. He had a life estate in the real estate of the wife. Most people would feel that this was not justice to the wife and that, therefore, it was contrary to the moral law. However, this law was changed in no state until a law was passed in Illinois in 1861 allowing a wife to have and own property after marriage, provided she brought the property into the marriage. She was moreover allowed to acquire and own property during her marriage provided she acquired it from someone other than her husband. This was the beginning of the liberalization of the laws in this country so far as women and their property rights are concerned.[41]

The point of this consideration of American law is that there has to be justice before the fullness of love can be realized. A husband is so constituted after the Fall that he uses his wife for his own pleasure until he gives consideration to the order of creation and renders justice. God's taking hold of a man makes him aware of his own selfishness and his need to render justice and love.

A real family is the perfect example of the cooperation of love and justice, of the ethics of the person and the ethics of the institution. Love creates the relationship of equality in the family, but that love must take a different form of expression in the father, the mother, and the child. That form is determined by justice. The father and the child know the need for authority on the part of the father and obedience on the part of the child, and only the spoiled child feels this is an infringement of freedom. The father who does not have authority along with love does not really love the child.[42] The mother is the natural mediator between the authority of the father and the love which flows freely, which is bound by no justice and no law. She can perform this function because she is not immediately responsible for the order of justice. She does not have to consider the authority that maintains familial justice, whereas the father does.[43]

Summary

The basis of marriage in Kant is contract for use. The principles that determine marriage are legislated by the practical reason in accordance with the juridical laws of pure reason.

Monogamy is based on rational argument. Rational argument also determines the rules governing the relationship of parents and child.

Kant did seek in his thought to make husband and wife equal and to make the relationship between husband and wife, parents and child responsible. One is always impressed, however, with the impersonal and logical way it is done. However, inadequate one might feel rational solutions are, Kant deserves praise because he succeeded more nearly than any another philosopher.

Brunner saw marriage as the order laid down by God in creation. Each partner is equal in the marriage. Yet each partner has a different function. The child is part of the reason we have been created sexual creatures. The other reason is that sex draws the couple together in the mutual expression of love. The parents are responsible to use their sex according to God's purpose. This does not imply that planning in marriage is forbidden, but only that planning must be done in a responsible manner.

The relation in the family is hierarchal: father, mother, and child. Each has his rights and each his parenthood and dignity. Love creates the relationship of equality in the family, but loves takes a different form of expression in father, mother, and child. That form is determined by justice. The father is responsible for this justice and authority, the mother for mediation between father and child. She symbolizes the love in the familial relationship which flows freely.

Endnotes

1. Kant, *The Philosophy of Law*, p. 109.
2. Ibid., p. 110.
3. Loc. cit.
4. Ibid., p. 111.
5. Ibid., p. 112.
6. Harry Sanger Richards, "Contracts," *American Law and Procedure*, Vol. I, p. 135.
7. Lindsay v. Smith, 78 N. C. 328. Ibid., p. 136.
8. Kant, *The Philosophy of Law*, p. 112.
9. Ibid., p. 113.
10. Cairns, *Legal Philosophy from Plato to Hegel*, p. 436.
11. Ibid., p. 116.
12. Albert Martin Kales, "Domestic Relations," *American Law and Procedure*, Vol. II, p. 374.
13. Kant, op. cit., p. 117.
14. Kant, *The Philosophy of Law*, p. 117.

15. Kales, op. cit., p. 366.
16. Kant, op. cit., p. 119.
17. Ibid., p. 119.
18. Ibid., p. 120. It is interesting to note that Kant's old servant Lamp was well treated. Instead of Kant's misuse of him it is suspected that Lamp beat Kant and ran away. Kant, in spite of the right he may have had to have Lamp brought back and punished, did nothing about the incident, though he never wished to speak of Lamp after that.
19. It ought to be emphasized that throughout this whole section on Kant and right or justice Kant is emphasizing the principles of right that make for justice. Law was for him the ordering of the various areas of society, according to the laws of reason or the moral law.
20. It is interesting to note in this relation that Kant according to Gierke, expressly attacked the welfare state. Gierke held this position because Kant held that impersonal right must be carried into effect regardless of persons. There was the further teaching that happiness could not be a factor unless it was intended as a means of ultimately securing a system of right. Gierke, op. cit., p. 308.
21. Brunner, *The Divine Imperative*, p. 375.
22. Paul Tillich in 1956 in *The Religious Situation* saw the separation of marriage from the Protestant idea of responsibility. At the time, he was writing from the point of view of socialism. He blamed capitalism for separating marriage from divine law and making it mere social convention. The revolt against bourgeois morality led to unregulated sexual instinct leading where it would. pp. 135-136.
23. Brunner, *The Divine Imperative*, p. 341.
24. Ibid., p. 347.
25. Ibid., p. 350.
26. Kant, *The Philosophy of Law*, p. 110.
27. Brunner, *The Divine Imperative*, p. 351.
28. Kant, *Eternal Peace*, p. 443.
29. Kant, *The Philosophy of Law*, p. 111.
30. Brunner, *The Divine Imperative*, p. 348.
31. Ibid., p. 349. The Biblical command is "Be fruitful and multiply."

Gen. 8:17. On the other hand, Berdyáev says of *eros* without the God-relationship, "There is eros as a demon and man can be possessed by him." *Slavery and Freedom*, p. 225. Berdyáev does not, however, make enough use of *eros* from the Christian point of view. After all, God made man and behold, he was very good. Gen. 1:31.

32. Matt. 19:6.
33. Brunner, *Justice and the Social Order*, p. 127.
34. I Cor. 7:4. Brunner cites this passage in his *Justice and the Social Order*, p. 128.
35. Brunner, *Justice and the Social Order*, p. 128.
36. Ibid., p. 129.
37. Ibid., p. 149.
38. Gen. 1:28.
39. Ibid., p. 130.
40. Ibid., p. 130.
41. Albert Martin Kales, "Domestic Relations and Persons", *American Law and Procedure*, Vol. II, p. 324.
42. Brunner, *Justice and the Social Order*, p. 131.
43. Ibid., p. 132.

CHAPTER VIII

Theory of the State

INTRODUCTION

Brunner has noted that on the Continent it is an undeniable fact that law means law of the state, and the jurists consider the state to be the only source of law.[1] It has always been otherwise in England and the United States. For in these countries the common law is independent of the state[2] and hardly distinguishable from social custom. But this common law can exist only so long as there is a close relation between law and morality.[3]

There is then an important distinction between the Continental view of the state, which views the state as the source of all law, and the English view, which sees law as independent of the state. Roman civil law came to recognize the emperor as a source of law. His power to issue edicts has influenced Continental civil law on this point. The English common law has taken a different view of the source of law. This was the point of argument between Coke and James I. James, who had been educated on the Continent and in Scotland, could not understand why he could not issue law and understand law as well as the English common law lawyers.[4]

Since Kant knew and greatly admired some aspects of the English government, and since Brunner attended school in the United States and taught at Princeton Seminary and other places, it can be assumed that in some measure there was familiarity with the English concept of law and the state on the part of both Brunner and Kant. The division of powers in government has had its more perfect development in English law. This was one thing that Kant admired about the English system. As noted above, Brunner has recognized the value of the English independence of law and its close tie with morality. Since English common law has been so influential in the world, and since it has such close ties with basic morality, it will be good to take a brief view of its development.

The background for American law is the English common law. The common law had its beginning when Henry II set up the royal curia, the king's court. There had been shire courts before, but they had been engrossed in the local and the particular interests of nobles and clerics and were never able to develop any system of law.

Henry II had foreign training in the law. Along with this real ability he knew how to choose men. He set up a royal bench of traveling judges who, along with intellectual children of later reigns, evolved the common law as fast as new precedents were set forth and recorded. These results were carried to various parts of the country by judges who went to the various shires. The English common law was not from the Code of Justinian, as was the civil law on the Continent. It was rather a labyrinth of precedents, cases, and decisions of the various royal courts. Its logic was learned and unravelled by the help of the legal profession.[5]

Statute law, or law passed by the legislature, began under Edward I. These laws altered the very substance of the law. Much of the law has been Anglo-Saxon, much of it local customs, and a great deal of it obsolete. The two basic elements of the common law were now set on their way: the unwritten law of precedents and the modifications by the legislative branch of the government.[6]

The Prerogative Courts would have set up Roman civil law in England. As has been noted already, the civil law has always been willing to exalt the power of the sovereign, there is such a strong tradition of the sovereign's being the source of law. This was the battle that Edward Coke fought with James I. With the civil law, the state was itself the source of law, and law was what the state determined it should be. The rights of the people were such rights as were granted. The common law reflected the moral outlook of the people as it had taken hold in their customs and in the men who had gone to Parliament and enacted laws. Since the rights of Parliament had been won from the power of the king over a long period of time, the common law carried within itself a semi-independence of royal power. This the House of Commons was quick to see under the leadership of Coke and others. The common law was a guarantor of the rights of Parliament and the people against the power of the king. Parliament won its victory in two main stages: the beheading of Charles I and the Bloodless Revolution of 1688.[7]

This battle had to be fought out, for there could no longer be two sets of laws in England. James I and Charles I with their Continental background in the civil law saw the judges as "lions under the Throne." The judges were the King's men and were bound to do his bidding. Coke, with the love of the common law in his veins, whatever other faults he may have had, conceived the law as having an independent status. The people and the king alike were under the law. He thought that laws could be changed, not by edicts of the king, but by the High Court of Parliament.[8]

Kant and Brunner on Liberty

Hendel thought that Kant became interested in politics because he was stirred by the American Revolution. It is known that Kant read Rousseau and loved him greatly and that even when it was most unpopular to do so, Kant spoke out in favor of the French Revolution.[9]

Although Kant admired the Roman civil law and recognized it as the highest embodiment of the juridical reason of the ancient world and expounded his own thought by constant reference to it, he saw its limitations. He did use it and sought to unfold through its categories the juridical ideas in their ultimate purity.[10]

Doubtless the thing that appealed to Kant in the Roman civil law was its reasoned approach. Kant was too individualistic to ever seriously burden the people with the tyranny of an absolute ruler. There are passages in Kant where he advised obedience to the ruler, even under the most trying circumstances.[11] However, his main emphasis is a union of peoples under just law. He suggested that justice comes from the people and emphasized the importance of the will of the people.[12]

Brunner's criticism of Kant questioned the rationalistic individualism. He is Swiss and his people have a long tradition of freedom. He does not disagree with Kant on any point concerning the liberty of the people. His basis for the grounding of these rights is different. All rights of man come from God and without God there are no rights.[13] God, in creating man, defines what belongs to man by right. "This and that belongs to man's life; this and that must not be taken away from him. Man has a claim to this and that because I have created him."[14]

Freedom may be said to be a "second word" then, but it is important because the first word is God. Freedom is rooted and grounded in God. It is our nature to be free. This freedom enables us to develop civilization and law.

Man has an eternal, inalienable right to freedom. Man has rights against the state. His right to have a voice in the affairs of the state comes from his equal rights with others and the dignity of his origin. The right to own property is important to Brunner, because without property there is no personal life nor any real freedom to act.[15]

Since law, justice, and freedom have no meaning outside of society, it is necessary to look at what Kant and Brunner have to say specifically about the state, which is the final center of earthly power for society in any particular region.

The State

Kant

Kant on the State

According to Kant, the relation of people to each other in a nation constitutes the civil union in the social state. Viewed from the point of view of the whole to its constituent members, there is formed the political state. The state is constituted by all for a just union. If a large proportion of the population participate, it is called a commonwealth. The principle of right in this sphere constitutes the national right. Viewed from the point of view of other than members of the particular state, this right will be viewed as a power. Considered by the inhabitants and their children this ordered coercion will be called a nation.[16]

Before the establishment of the state, men exercised violence against each other. This condition of men, before the ideal of rational right took hold, made a war of all against all. Man had to leave the state of nature where each did what was pleasing to himself. Under the social contract, men agreed to accept compulsory laws. They then began to live in a civil union in which each has by law what should be his.[17]

It need not be assumed that chaos was absolute in the state of nature. If there ever had been such a condition, there would have been no one to serve as a competent judge in the chaos to bring order out of the chaos in which man would have found himself. Man had need for law as a means of bringing order in the matter of who owned what; otherwise a man could own only what he could physically restrain. The condition of the state of nature of the mine and thine is carried over into civil law and enforced.[18]

According to Kant, every state has three powers: the legislative, the executive, and the judicial. The legislative power of the sovereign state is in the person of the lawgiver. In a democracy, the lawmaking power is in the legislature. As a rational principle, the legislative power of the state belongs to the people.[19] If one individual determines anything in contradistinction from another, it is possible that he can perpetuate a wrong on the other person, but this is never possible when all determine what the law will be. Hence the legislative power ought to take in the will of all the people.[20]

The citizen possesses three rights which belong inseparably to him. They are as follows: 1. Constitutional freedom. The citizen has to obey no other laws than the ones to which he gives his consent. 2. Civil equality. This is the right to recognize no one superior to oneself except as that person has moral power to impose obligation. There is a mutuality of imposing such obligation. I impose such obligation on my neighbor and he can do the same upon me. 3. Political independence.[21] This is the right one has to owe one's existence and continuance in society not to the arbitrary will of another but to one's own right and powers as a member of the commonwealth. The citizen consequently possesses a civil personality which cannot be represented by anyone but himself. Kant excludes apprentices, servants, women, and all who are compelled to maintain themselves under the control of others. In other words, he excludes the wage earners, and in accord with his time, women. One might exempt woodcutters and ploughmen from civil personality, but one is surprised to find tutors in this group. Kant explained that they are to be excluded because they are too excessively controlled by those for whom they work. Therefore, he reasoned that they would have no independence of their own. All this group are passive subjects, but they are to be treated by the citizens according to the laws of freedom and equality that govern them.[22]

The act by which the people made themselves into a state is termed the original contract. Each and all of the people give up their external freedom to receive it back again as members of the commonwealth. The commonwealth is the people viewed as welded into a state. An individual has not sacrificed a part of his freedom to be a part of the state; rather he has but given up his wild lawlessness to find his proper freedom. His rights are undiminished but regulated by right. This position of dependence arises out of his own regulative lawgiving will.

The executive power belongs to the head of the state, whether this be in the person of a king or prince. The executive authority appoints the magistrates, and promulgates laws enacted by the legislature. A government having the executive and the legislative power in one person would be a despotic government. The governor should be the administrator standing under the law enacted by the legislature. The legislative power may deprive the governor of his power, but it may not punish him. Punishment ought to be by the executive.

The executive ought not exercise the judicial power himself but appoint magistrates. The sovereign should not act as a judge, for this would put him in a position where he might do wrong. In a real sense it is the people who can alone judge a case, but they do it indirectly through representatives elected by them. What Kant had in mind here is primarily that the people judge themselves through their juries.[23]

The supreme head in the state has only rights and no compulsory duties toward the subjects. There is no law allowing for resistance to the head of the state, for whoever would resist the head of the state, logically, would make himself equal to the head of the state and this would be contradictory. Resistance is at no time justified, for to allow such resistance would be contrary to the nature of the state which has to be by nature coercive to keep order. The people have no right of rebellion, but rather they should bear what is laid upon them though conditions seem unbearable.[24]

It must be admitted that Kant does not seem to be logical at this point, for he holds that the sovereignty is in the people and is inalienable. If the general will decreed a change, it is not clear why the sovereign power cannot be changed. Granted the sovereign may be a corporate personality, just why corporations may not be dissolved is not clear. It may be that Kant's argument is a purely logical one; the state as the sovereign head cannot be destroyed, since it is the nature of the state to order society. This must be the case, for Kant went on to say that defective constitutions may be altered. This should be done by the sovereign power in the way of reform rather than by way of revolution. The real sovereign power in the state is in the legislature and it may resist the executive. The British were wrong in cutting off Charles I's head. Yet once a government has been established, whether wrongly as Kant thought in the case of the Cromwell government, or rightly as he seems to have felt in the case of the American Revolution, the people have to obey it as good citizens.[25]

Principles of Government

In his work *Theory and Practice*, Kant sets forth what he thought a governmental constitution should contain. It is an able exposition on the just state and what it should be. He believed that a good government would have public laws so that every man could live and be secure against the interference of every other man. He did not believe that happiness was a satisfactory ground for determining external right.[26]

It is true that harmonization of wills makes for freedom at least on a limited, but only possible, scale. Yet Kant thought that government is based on coercion, since there are governing principles that are rational and right:

1. The freedom of each member of a society as a man.
2. The equality of each member with every other as a subject.
3. The autonomy of each member of a commonwealth as a citizen.[27]

These are principles by which the state could be organized. The freedom of man ought to be a principle for the constitution of a commonwealth. A patriotic commonwealth is concerned with men capable of enjoying their rights. No man can coerce another except through public law enforced by the head of the government. Each man has the right to protection against undue coercion unless he has legally lost that right by committing a crime. No man can lose the equality he has in the commonwealth except through crime which may deprive him of his right. A man cannot even contract to give up this right; for a man cannot give up being master of himself. This does not affect what has been said about certain subjects not having voting rights as citizens.[28] At the same time, a big property owner has only one vote even as the small property owner. The prerequisite for voting is owning property.[29]

The welfare of the group has to be considered before the welfare of individuals or special groups. Kant believed that the welfare of individuals, if that was all that was desired, could best be attained in a state of nature. The best for all is where there is the greatest agreement and coordination between the constitution and right.

The reason men do not have better government is because they do not use their reason to provide better standards. Men prefer what they have rather than risk the danger of trying the new. Reason would point the way if men would use it. Constitutional law should be based on reason, since right is taught by reason rather than experience.[30]

Brunner

Background Principles on the Source of Law

Much has been written since the First World War about the "irresponsibles." The irresponsibles were those who were occupied with economic ideas without regard to their implications. Much of this protest was about those who had accepted Marxian ideas without the thought of consequences. Undoubtedly many of the economic interpretations of history were in this category. Professors, who would have thought it unsophisticated and unpardonable to give a student a Bible, gave copies of Marx's works to their students with the implied endorsement of their learning and standing in the university. Unfortunately, it was not only the intellectual Marxians who were in this sense irresponsibles; yet it was this group which proved the most dangerous, and if not dangerous, at least the most maligned and not without desert. Many of these men were intellectually toying with ideas which seemed clever but which they had no intention of carrying out in practice. Their students took the ideas seriously with tragic results.

Such seems to have been the case with two jurists who lived and wrote even before Marxism was dreamed of. They would have hated the use to which their ideas were put. Their ideas were conducive to the power of the state's being supreme. The two men under consideration are Austin and Kelsen. Austin, who lived in England in the first half of the nineteenth century, taught that law is a precept addressed to the community. With goodness or badness of law as tested by utility, the jurist has no concern. Law is imposed and enforced by the sovereign. Austin was not indifferent to justice but saw it as a pre-legal question only. The jurist sees principles as abstracted from positive systems so the exposition of such principles is its exclusive object.[31]

There can be no doubt that there is an indifference to religion and ethics as it relates to the source of law and the justice of laws in Austin's system. Michlem rightly stated that law should be more than "a mere aggregation of rules." It has to be an expression of justice and right. There is "a deadly peril involved in the treatment of scientific abstractions as if they covered the whole field in all of its aspects."[32]

Hans Kelsen lived in the early part of this century in Germany. He exerted great influence standing for law in its pure form, law uncontaminated by any infusion of sociology or ethics or theology or politics. Kelsen was not concerned with the philosophical principle of justice as such. He thought of it as "an irrational idea." In the German idiom this meant nonrational or nonlogical. Good or bad laws, just or unjust laws are no concern of jurisprudence, he thought. Law is a science concerned exclusively with the norms or standards set up in various legal systems, and these in their turn derive from some basic norm or constitution, the validity of which is the hypothesis. Kelsen's concern was logical consistency with some basic norm which would be morally, culturally, or aesthetically neutral.[33]

It should not take much thought or imagination to see that with the religious aspect left out of consideration, the source of the law proceeding from the sovereign and the only concern of law being logical consistency, much of the ground work is laid for the modern totalitarian state. The jurist Eherling said, "The state is the sole source of law." Jellinek arrived at the same conclusion.[34]

Brunner thought that law would perish if the views of the abovementioned formalistic thinkers on jurisprudence were to get the upper hand in the legal thought of the people, views in which law has nothing whatever to do with justice, but merely a matter of convenience, frictionless procedure, or formal logic.[35]

Brunner on the State

The rise of Hitler and the Second World War brought to Brunner's attention the problem of justice as it relates itself to natural law and the order of creation. The modern states which followed the lead of the positivistic jurists, for example, Eherling, have emphasized the state as the sole source of law from which there is no appeal. There was a tradition in the medieval period in the civil law countries which allowed the ruler to be the source of law; however, this was always limited by the natural law which taught that laws contrary to the law of nature could be disobeyed. Rulers were also supposed to be Christian; however, it must be admitted that often this did not do much in the way of amelioration. In any case, the techniques of state control were not available to the medieval monarch, techniques which have made the modern state so fearful a thing because of the possibility of the control of all the modern media of propaganda. There are the additional means of wire tapping and other dangerous practices which amount to real thought control.

At least the totalitarian state served to remind modern man that there are not only primal rights for individuals and communities, but also there is a just and a unique order of the state itself. The totalitarian state absorbs all institutions and all rights.[36] This is the inevitable outcome of the view of the state's not being subject to natural law, but rather that it establishes as law whatever it approves, and that all rights obtaining among the people issue from a state center.[37]

Brunner believed that statism takes over whenever the principle of federalism, the building of the community from below, has been done away with. Federalism is forced upon man because it is the antithesis of all power in the super-state. Federalism does not make the state the supreme value. It keeps in perspective the truth that the state is made for man and not man for the state. This principle of federalism is according to God's order of creation. It is in accordance with man's freedom and enables man better to hear God's call as it goes to individuals; for only individuals hear and respond. Only the individual has a conscience and a sense of responsibility. Whenever individuals are spoken of as "collective persons," the totalitarian lie has taken over.[38] Brunner is afraid that the idea of collective personality would always lead to totalitarianism. He believes that the individual must be asserted over the collective.

The individual is called into love which has its true substance in a life of fellowship. This is an individual relationship to God in which no questions of rights or systems are asked. Every man owes his existence to being a part of a community. The local community is more important to a man in his normal living than the state, but it is the family that is the prototype of every community. This is in contrast to what the totalitarian state likes to think, for it desires to take all power unto itself.

No state can, much as the totalitarian state wills to do so, formulate laws of marriage. The totalitarian state "abolishes" marriage, or does what it wills according to its own will, but in doing so it violates the order of creation and shows its own injustice. Conversely, a state is just when it lays stress on the law which is independent of it.[39]

The family is the prototype of the ideal community, and its rights take precedence over those of the state. However, the family is not the only community whose rights take precedence over those of the state. Between the family and the state there exists in the order of creation a host of intermediate links. These are necessary to life, but the state could conceivably be done away with and man continue to exist. The state is an integral part of human life in that there must be supreme, encompassing union of all the primary forms of community. The state has the monopoly of force and must take charge of everything that men do not do of their own accord. It may be possible for the state not to exist but men have to live and work together. This work covers the economic spheres. The state is the last link in the chain of these associations.[40]

Manners, customs, agreements, contracts, rites, and ceremonies are the standards of justice in these forms of community. The state in the first instance pays no attention to these. The state does not set these in motion, nor does it lay down the rules by which they proceed. The state comes later, protesting, preserving, regulating, but it does not come as a constitutive but as a regulative agent. It coordinates, protects, and supports by its coercive power.

The state always has a monopoly of coercive power extending to the extreme case of power over life and death. The state does what it alone can do because it has the power to coerce. It is at the same time the most embracing organization that the national group can know.[41]

Although Kant knew the principle of federalism, he did not apply it to the national state. It is the basis for his structure of world government, as can be seen from his work *Eternal Peace*. Kant seems to have felt that the guarantee of equal rights before the law could be guaranteed by constitutions, for Kant had great faith in constitutions.[42] Brunner criticized Kant for his individualistic conception of people and ruler, but he did recognize his contribution of the equality of citizens before the law.[43]

Brunner, unlike Kant who believed people could establish a good government, though devils worked against it, if only the people would use their reason, is pessimistic about the state. He taught that the Fall is the reason why the essence of the state is power rather than justice. The Fall has upset the finely proportioned intelligence that Kant believed so much in, so that the state is not nicely just but unjust. Yet it is still a state. Power is its essence. Strangely, this power is the thing that is so necessary to prevent anarchy and at the same time it is so easily corruptible; in fact, all power is corrupt to some extent.

The Christian is reluctant to bestow the name of state on the omnipotent power that has come into being in modern times. Nevertheless, it performs the functions of the state, and to refuse to give it the name would only mean that a new name would have to be invented for it.

The reason Brunner held so strongly to calling the modern "totalitarian state" by that name is the function that even absolute power performs. It at least keeps out the worse danger of anarchy, which can give no justice at all. The absolute state has to give justice at least to the point of keeping order.[44] In doing so, it provides some restraint to the wicked.[45]

Law is the first prerequisite of a good state. Even a dictatorship cannot long rule without setting up some law other than the personal will of the ruler. He may have set up law from a desire for the will to power, but something good will come of it. The law cannot help but create a certain determinate element of justice. The constancy of a legal rule enforced is a victory of mind over the mindlessness of wantonness and caprice.[46]

Of course, there is a difference between a just law and an unjust law. The just law as distinguished from an unjust law embodies the human rights of the individual and community as established by creation. "No juristic formalism and no historical argument against the law of nature can do away with the fact there are requirements of justice which it is the task of the just legislator to embody in laws."[47]

Every reader of the Bible knows the close relation that exists between law and the divine will. The concept of divine law is fundamental to Biblical thinking. It is clear that this "jus divinum" transcends all legal relations between men, being also the basis of purely moral and religious relations and conduct. However, when the jurists came to set up law in the Christian era, they found certain concepts which it seems possible to use. Justice, they reasoned, in contradistinction from love, is identical with "belonging" and this "belonging" was understood in a normative sense, independent of human law.

Justice presupposed a divine order of belonging no matter how this belonging is conceived to be. This, then, became the meaning of *lex naturae* both for the pre-Christian and for the Christian. This order of belonging was seen not to be an order of "nature in the pantheistic sense of the word but of God's creation. Understandably this thinking evolved over a period of time.[48]

For the Christian the *lex naturae* and the *lex creatoris* were never the final principle. They would be qualified by two concepts: the concept of the sovereignty of God, which stands above his law, and the love of God which administers the law. At the same time love seeks to overcome the law, for love seeks perfection and the perfect can never be merely just.[49]

Coercion is an important element in law, but there has to be respect for law, which contains a divine element which gives it a binding element. Positivism and class legislation have undoubtedly done damage to this element. When this respect is present, laws that are just are easier to enforce, but laws which are not just are sure to bring strong protest.[50]

This means that the basis of earthly justice of the legal order between men is God's creation of man, in so far as it includes those things which belong to man and yet could, though unjustly, be taken away from him by his fellow men. In other words, the *Christian concept of justice and law is based on the Christian conception of man.*[51]

Since the state is an impersonal power that can never be personal, it is not primarily a moral institution but a product of history. The Christian state never existed and never will exist. Where the state is concerned, applied ethics will always lag behind principle. Nevertheless, "...the state is at the same time an ethical body, since it arises through powerful actions in actual events and can only be affirmed for its ethical purpose. State action should always be placed under the divine command even though here the command cannot be anticipated in any kind of law."[52]

The kind of government is important in the makeup of the state. Democracy is the supreme limitation of the state's coercive power by the will of the people. The power of the state is so limited usually that it hardly appears as power. Yet it would have to be said that justice is more important than the question of democracy or lack of it. This can be seen when democracies set up and enforce bad laws.[53]

In modern times, the question of human rights has come to the fore. These rights precede the state, and the state has to acknowledge the truth that these "birthrights" of mankind are founded on God's creation.[54]

> It is this conception which distinguishes the lawful state from the totalitarian state. In the moment when these aboriginal human rights are denied or abolished by the state, the totalitarian state is there...The human rights precede the state in order of dignity. The state is created for the procreation of these human rights which man has not from the state but from the Creator...[55]

Niebuhr added a dimension of thought on the state, although it may be implicit in Brunner's thought. The element of self-interest plays a large part in the life of every nation. This was demonstrated during the last war when our own leaders were torn between (1) the expression of our war aims in terms of survival and (2) their expression as a fight for the universal and transcendent values. Every nation or state alleges to extend international justice while it pursues its own.[56] Yet every nation does embody values which transcend their mere existence.[57] Niebuhr admitted the attempt of nations to embody value, but pride asserts greater embodiment than is actually achieved. Every nation gives expression to its own self-interest, but the sense of justice and sense of fear make for a modification of this self-interest to a consideration of others and their needs to a limited extent.[58]

Summary

Kant may be regarded as a political liberal if one disregards certain passages in his political works. One may lay this to a necessity to please the ruler of his state, along with keeping his own conviction. On the other hand, one may do, as Gierke does, and lay this conservative aspect of Kant to Kant in real practice.[59]

Kant seems to have had a real belief in the people as sovereign. The government was to express as best it could the general will, for it gained its power through the general will. The government of the state was to have three departments of government: the executive, the legislative, and the judicial. By this separation justice was to be the better done.

Reason in its legislative capacity holds the state together for Kant and gives it its validity. For Brunner, reason plays its part, for justice works within the realm of the rational ordering, but the basis of the state and what makes it a just state is its adherence to the order of creation. The nature of man and God's sovereignty must be considered to have a just state. The natural law becomes normative and sets the just within the state. This norm is to give to each his due as a creature of God. For each man has rights which God has given to him.

Endnotes

1. In this country the common law is applied to the state and local government only. However it serves as the background for term definitions, etc. for the national government. The common law is independent of all branches of government to the extent that it evolves and is not enacted law, and, therefore, the will of the legislature.
2. Brunner, *Christianity and Civilization*, Vol. I, p. 106.
3. Ibid., p. 105.
4. G. M. Trevelyan, *Illustrated History of England*, p. 257.
5. Ibid., p. 258.
6. Ibid., p. 89.
7. Ibid., p. 391.
8. Ibid., p. 392.
9. C. W. Hendel, editor, *The Philosophy of Kant and Our Modern World*, p. 97.
10. W. Hastie, "Introduction," Kant's *The Philosophy of Law*, p. xii.
11. Kant, *The Philosophy of Law*, p. 177.
12. Ibid., p. 164.
13. Brunner, *Christianity and Civilization*, Vol. 1, p. 117.
14. Ibid., Part 2, p. 109. J. Edgar Hoover wrote this about communism as he has studied it and sought to stamp it out in this country as head of the F.B.I. He saw this to be the case under communism. The individual is not a creature of God, loved and cherished, but a blotch of skin and bones to be trained, manipulated, and exploited for reasons of state. Love, mercy, and justice become meaningless symbols, mocked as "bourgeois weakness." The state becomes supreme and man exists to serve a supreme master whose every whim is final and irrevocable. Man becomes a tool without personality or individuality. In other words, our Judeo-Christian history is completely reversed. J. Edgar Hoover,

"Communism: The Bitter Enemy of Religion," *Christianity Today*, Vol. III, No. 19, June 22, 1955.

15. Brunner, *Justice and the Social Order*, p. 58.
16. Kant, *The Philosophy of Law*, p. 161. Luthuli, an African chief who was deposed from his chieftainship by the South African Government, feels that the mission teaching he received (Christian teaching) gives him a sense of the dignity of man in the sight of God. His Christian belief also makes him feel that laws and conditions which debase man must be opposed in the spirit of defiance which St. Peter showed when he said of the rulers of his day, "We must obey God rather than man." Nadine Gordimer, "Chief Luthuli," *The Atlantic Monthly*, April 1959, p. 35.
17. Ibid., p. 164. Kant did not believe in a historical contract. Rather it was a logical postulate.
18. Ibid., p. 166.
19. Ibid., p. 166. When the holiness of the law or the voice of God's being known to the people is lost, Tillich is right in saying that the next state for those in government is to see their work as a profession rather than as a divine calling. *The Religious Situation*, p. 127.
20. Ibid., p. 166.
21. Bishop Gerald Kennedy of the Los Angeles Area of the Methodist Church in his article "Could It Happen Here?" gives a perfect example of what prevails where constitutional principles do not prevail. In South Africa the judges may render a decision but the Senate by a simple majority may reverse the decision or write a new law, which would amount to the same thing. As an example the Afrikaans Party has packed the Senate, and law trials involving negroes in any way have become a farce. This is true even where the judges are able men. Writing of a trial that Kennedy witnessed, he wrote, "What was wrong with the whole procedure? Simply that it was a farce and everybody knew it. If the government did not get the verdict it desired, it could set the judgement aside, change the law, or simply try another angle...When men destroy the sanctity of law and the authority of courts there is no place to stand. It is like playing a game without rules...The issue is whether we want to be governed by law. To leave the decision to men—even good men—would not be wise, for none are free from the influence of personal prejudices and emotional pres-

sures...In this contest, the Church needs to remember that a part of its Gospel is the good news of law." Kant would agree to this without much reservation. Gerald Kennedy "Could It Happen Here?" *The Christian Advocate*, February 4, 1960, p. 5.

22. Kant, *The Philosophy of Law*, p. 168. J. G. Meicklejohn hails as a great principle of civil liberties Kant's principle that man should live externally free as he lives conformable to the freedom of others. "Kantian Formalism and Civil Liberties," *Journal of Philosophy*, p. 843.
23. Ibid., pp. 172-173.
24. Ibid., p. 181. Meicklejohn has pointed out that this emphasis in Kant has always offended the Jeffersonian liberals. He admits that Kant does seem rather passive at this point, since his solution seems to be to appeal to philosophers to write against such evils. He does urge that men strive for rationality, and Meicklejohn feels this is the long time solution. He recognizes, however, that this is different from the Jeffersonian solution of the "right of the people to alter and abolish." Meicklejohn, "Kantian Formalism and Civil Liberties," *Journal of Philosophy*, December 1, 1954, p. 843.
25. Ibid., p. 181.
26. Kant, *Theory and Practice*, p. 415. Pound has pointed to the importance of Kant's principle: Right is the limitation of every man's freedom so that it harmonizes with the freedom of every other man. He saw this as one of the evidences of Kant's thought on other able philosophers of law. Pound, *The Spirit of the Common Law*, p. 8.
27. Kant, *Theory and Practice*, p. 416.
28. Ibid., p. 419.
29. Ibid., p. 421. Gierke pointed out that Kant was not a democrat in practice, and he pointed to the passages concerning the power of the sovereign. Many of them seem to be talking about the king or prince. Gierke, Natural Law, p. 354.
30. Kant, *Eternal Peace*, p. 456.
31. Nathaniel Michlem, *Law and Ethics*, p. 51.
32. Ibid., p. 52.
33. Ibid., p. 60.
34. Brunner, *Justice and the Social Order*, No. 79, p. 342.

35. Ibid., p. 185.

36. Berdyáev points to the medieval preservation of the rights of individuals in spite of the emphasis on authority. This was theory which was in practice abused in the hunts for heresy. Still he is convinced that medieval consciousness was superior to the Christian consciousness in our own day. *The Realm of the Spirit and the Realm of Caesar*, p. 77.

37. Brunner, *Justice and the Social Order*, p. 120.

38. Ibid., p. 121. Although Brunner praised the English system most highly for this independence in *Christianity and Civilization*, Part 2, p. 113, he holds up his own Swiss law system as ideal in *Justice and the Social Order*, p. 189.

39. A state may not abolish marriage, but it may regulate marriage in accordance with the faith of the community and state. In the struggle with the Mormons over polygamy, the Supreme Court of the United States in Davis v. Boston in 1890 stated, "Bigamy and polygamy are crimes by the laws of all civilized and Christian countries...To extend exceptions from punishment for such crimes would be to shock the moral judgment of the community." Quoted by Merrimon Cunninggim, *Freedom's Holy Light*, p. 65. There can be no doubt that Christianity and the Western civilization, which purports to be Christian, take for public law and policy the standards of Christian morality.

40. Ibid., p. 122. Berdyáev sees Caesar as trying to take to himself not only what belongs to him, but also what belongs to God. Caesar wishes to subject the whole of man to himself. The state attempts to serve Caesar; it makes man only a statistical unit. When the state becomes interested in man, it enslaves him. Caesar for Berdyáev is the symbol of the finite and the evil. Berdyáev, The *Realm of the Spirit and the Realm of Caesar*, p. 79. Berdyáev sees something of the fallen nature of the state. Since he was driven out of Russia by the communists after having aided in establishing the revolution, he knew from hard experience the enslaving nature of the state without God.

41. Ibid., p. 123.

42. Kant, Friedrich, editor, *Eternal Peace*, p. 453.

43. Brunner, *Justice and the Social Order*, p. 41. Brunner's criticism of Kant's individualism is partly concerned with the fact that Kant

did not recognize the inequalities along with the equalities, but this is not too cogent a criticism. The whole argument ought to have been centered on isolated individuals before the ruler. Family and groups in community are not considered.

44. Ibid., p. 175.
45. Ibid., p. 176.
46. Ibid., p. 177.
47. Ibid., p. 178. The common law has embodied Christian teaching in much of its more liberal rulings. In the case of People v. Bugles, James Kent held that Christianity was recognized by the law, therefore blasphemy against God and profane ridicule of Christ or the Holy Scriptures are punishable at common law. The people of this state, in common with the people of this country, profess the general doctrines of Christianity, as the rule of their faith and practice; and, to scandalize the author of these doctrines is not only, in a religious point of view extremely impious, but even in respect to the obligation due to society, is a gross violation of decency and good order. Merrimon Cunninggim, *Freedom's Holy Light*, p. 66.
48. Brunner, *Christianity and Civilization*, Part II, p. 109.
49. Brunner, *The Divine Imperative*, p. 449.
50. Ibid., p. 451.
51. Brunner, *Christianity and Civilization*, p. 110.
52. Brunner, *The Divine Imperative*, p. 463.
53. Brunner, *Justice and the Social Order*, p. 111.
54. Eduard Heimann has noted that justice is more important than democracy, although he does not depreciate democracy. He also notes the state's turning to its own law, which is power, when religious authority is withdrawn. This was true in Germany where there was no humanizing, liberating tendency and no moral principle to check the will to power. *What the Christian can Contribute Toward a Better World*, editor Bishop William Scarlette, essay noted, "Man and the State" by Eduard Heimann, p. 97.
55. Brunner, *Christianity and Civilization*, Part 2, p. 111.
56. Niebuhr, *Moral Man In Immoral Society*, p. 96.
57. Niebuhr, *The Nature and Destiny of Man*, Vol. I, p. 213.

58. Niebuhr, *Discussion Outline and Work Paper*, February 1956. Reinhold Niebuhr seems to be not too far from Bentham in his doctrine of self-interest. Bentham takes the doctrine much further, however. On Bentham, see Halevy, *The Growth of Philosophic Radicalism*, p. 15.
59. Gierke, *Natural Law*, p. 330. It seems likely that Kant had to satisfy his ruler. One ought not be too hard on him for this necessity.

CHAPTER IX

Some Principles of International Law and Justice

Introduction

There is little doubt that people today are thinking more about international law than once was the case. The fact that Edward R. Murrow would devote one program of "Small World" to the subject would seem to indicate a mounting interest and concern.[1]

Brendon F. Brown has in our time reminded us that international justice is a mandate of the natural law. It determines and defines the duties of the states in mutual relations and dealing. Natural law has to have a greater place in international law than in national law, especially where there is no positive precedent to come to bear on the particular case.[2]

Arnold Hall, writing a generation earlier for students interested in the law, did not feel this pressing modern need for a method to rid ourselves of anarchy. In any case, he probably was sticking strictly to law as a fact when he wrote, "International law is that body of rules which civilized nations have accepted as binding upon them in their relations with one another."[3]

Brunner and other writers might look to a transcendent perspective from which men are led to accept or reject agreements. Hall apparently would not have it that way, for he went on to write,

> Many writers in defining international law define it as having its source in reason or justice, implying that what is right or just between nations is the law of nations. Here there is evident confusion. The rules which civilized nations accept are the rules of international law, regardless of their moral or rational quality.[4]

Hall doubtless was right so far as there have been precedents to cover cases, for there are wide areas which remain unsettled and for which no precedent can yet be found. To better understand the principles involved it is good to examine what Kant and Brunner have to say on the subject.

KANT

To Seek Peace a Duty

Kant once confessed that nowhere did human nature appear less attractive than in the relation of whole nations to each other.[5] Yet he had faith in the ability of men to set up constitutional government so that it would work. "The problem of establishing a state is solvable even for a people of devils, if only they have intelligence."[6] Kant once admitted to a friend that his works on peace were "reveries on peace."[7] He saw that the "event depends upon freedom" and few minds would dare draw the line or at any time give up hope. He saw that "to seek peace is a duty."[8] It is part of man's striving toward his own freedom. The moral will counts in the last analysis. The moral man, when he conceives of the law that imposes its obligation knows it as an absolute universal principle. He cannot think of himself in any other way than under obligation. This means that it cannot be limited to his own nation. It has to apply to all humanity.[9]

The practical implementation for peace is international law and justice. This aim is not to be realized in any near future time. But if there is ground for hope, it will be a long time before it will be realized. Then lasting peace can be seen as no empty dream. Still the vision gives us a task to perform.[10] Friedrich saw Kant as the one major philosopher of the Golden Age of European philosophy who never wavered in his working for peace. Although this seems a little extreme, he went so far as to say that Kant dealt with the problem as a major interest in all more important works. It is known that Kant saw as one of his basic truths (categorical imperatives), "There shall be no war."[11]

Kant started his discussion of international law with what it will cover.

> The public right of states in their relation to one another...Wherever a state viewed as a moral person acts in relation to another existing in the condition of natural freedom, and consequently in a state of continual war, such right takes its rise.[12]

The right of nations to the state of war may be divided into

1. The right of going to war.
2. Right during war.
3. Right after war.

This latter aim is to constrain the nations mutually to pass from a state of war to a state of peace. Yet the natural state of man was in the state of nature war. The rights of the strong prevailed in this natural state. Going to war is asserting the right to revert as nations to this condition. Yet Kant would lay down rules for war. As to the right to go to war and rights during war, suffice it to say that Kant allows the first as a reversion to the state of nature; the second he approached as humanely as possible. He wanted the war to work toward right, condoning no war of extermination or of subjugation of a whole people.[13]

Rights After War

The rights of a peace treaty begin after the signing. The conqueror sets up terms to which he will agree. The conqueror may not demand the cost of fighting the war, because in doing so he would be declaring the war on the part of the opponent to be unjust. The next thing will be exchange of prisoners which ought to be done with equity of numbers.

The citizens of a conquered state do not lose their citizenship rights upon their state's being conquered, nor does the conquered state, for that matter, lose its national citizenship, so to speak. To allow otherwise would be to make the conquered country into a colony of the conqueror, and the citizens would be degraded to slaves.

Slavery cannot be shown to be a rightful institution from conquest of a people in war, for this would be a punitive war which is wrong. Even with more force Kant wanted it said that hereditary slavery as a result of war is wrong. This would assume inherited criminality which is not right, since guilt cannot be inherited. Rather, an amnesty should be given at the setting up of the peace treaty. This is, moreover, implied in the very idea of peace.[14]

> The rights of peace are as follows:
> 1.The right to be at peace when the war is in the neighboring state. A state has also the right to be neutral.
> 2.The right to have peace secured in such a way that there may be genuine peace when it is concluded.
> 3.The right of several states to enter into an alliance when there is the desire to do so. This does not mean that it can be used for an aggression of any kind.[15]

The rights of peace are important, but while war is being waged against an unjust enemy all reasonable means may be used to win the war. These things may be done to keep what is a state's own property and protect the citizens in their property. An unjust nation is one whose publicly expressed will, whether in word or deed, betrays a maxim which, if it were taken as a universal rule, would make a state of peace among the nations impossible and would perpetuate the state of nature. Such wrong would be the violation of a peace treaty.

The Value of Nature and History

Kant believed that the "evil principle" in men could be in a state of control so that society could be ordered for the good of all. By analogy, he believed that a civil society could be set up which would order the disorder of nations in their chaotic condition. Kant recognized that writing a constitution was not enough. There had to be a desire for peace, and intelligence had to rule to establish or maintain a lawful relation among states. This would be brought about by nature in using the quarrelsomeness of men to make them want to find a condition of quiet and security.[16] Nature can use the desire to be free from the endless preparation for war to create a desire for peace. In using man's weariness of war, she is but pointing up what reason would have told men in the first place. If they had listened to reason, they would have been delivered from the many sad experiences they have known. Reason would have liked to point up the need for a union of nations, wherein even the smallest can have security and its rights. This would come from the fact that they would have strength in union. It is from a desire to escape inevitable destruction that men will be driven to seek security through a lawful constitution. This will be hard for "the wild man" who will be reluctantly forced to give up his "brutal" freedom.[17]

Nature has a providential plan to lead men to a better way, through men's reason if they will, but through the brutal lessons of history if they will not. Nature intends to bring about a new relation between states. In some cases, the old states will be broken up and new states established which can maintain themselves. Nature will in time evolve constitutional commonwealths which can maintain themselves. Thus nature uses the wild disorder of men to bring about good, even though the situation looks hopeless and all men seem about to be destroyed. That nature is reasonable is a certitude. She guarantees that such good will will come. Nature is now moving events to this appropriate end.[18]

Men in the past have let war keep them so occupied that they have not fully realized the use of their rational capacities. They will have to be awake, however, to the dangers that security may lull them to sleep and so not be on their toes to develop their mental activities, as they should. It would appear that Kant was under no illusion about a stalemate because of the lack of war, for he saw that this would come only with a league that was a sound federation. He saw that every pretended good must be grafted upon every morally good frame of mind. If it is not so grafted, it is a pretense, a glittering misery. "Mankind will probably remain in this condition until, as I have said, it has struggled out of the chaotic condition of the relations among states."[19]

The history of mankind, Kant thought, is a hidden plan of nature which, in order to bring about better conditions, must rely on the evolutionary process and reason. What matters in seeking this hidden plan of nature is to see if some progress is revealed. There is such a small part of the plan revealed to date that it is not clear the course the evolution will take or the relation of the parts to the whole. It is the nature of man to look to the future with hope, if only some sudden gleam is revealed with certainty. States are now in an insecure relation one to another. Kant hoped men would tire of the restrictions on trade and commerce that war brings and would work for peace. Enlightenment is a good which must ever draw mankind from the egoistic expansive tendencies of its rulers once they understand their own advantage. Along with all else, the practical reminder of the large war debt would make people seek peace.[20]

A Federal World Government

The achievement of peace is the first big step for nations to seek. When it comes to setting up the form the constitution ought to take, both for the state and for the world federation, the best constitution is republican. A republican constitution will be founded upon these three principles: 1. the principle of freedom of all members of a society as men; 2. the principle of the dependence of all upon a single common legislation as subjects; 3. the principle of the equality of all the citizens. This is the only type of constitution which is derived from the idea of an original contract upon which all rightful legislation of a nation must be based.[21]

Kant had real hope that a republican constitution would work for eternal peace. A king might start a war quickly when he does not wish to consider others' wishes so far as costs are concerned, whereas a republican constitution would allow the citizen to vote for or against war. The citizenry will not lightly vote for war when there will be restrictions, deprivation, want, and great destruction of property.[22]

As to the best method of achieving world government, Kant thought a federation, a congress of nations, would be the best way.[23] He believed this federation to be a right. He wrote, "This right, in so far as it relates to a possible union of all nations in respect to certain laws universally regulating their intercourse with each other, may be called 'cosmopolitical right.'"[24]

Kant thought citizens ought to be able to travel. A member of one state does not have a right against another state to visit its territory, but, Kant thought, this arrangement should be worked out in the federation, for "a citizen of the world" should attempt to enter into communion with the people of other regions and visit them.[25]

Since men render homage to the concept of law, Kant thought that this proved that there exists in man a greater moral quality (although a dormant one) to try to master the evil element in him. This "evil nature" has been held in check by the national state government, but it seems to have free play among nations. Nevertheless, he held that reason speaks from the throne of the highest legislative power and condemns war as a method of finding what is right. Reason makes the achievement of peace a direct duty. Reason demands that something be done to establish a peace treaty, but this must be more than the usual peace treaty. It must set up a world union. This union is not directed toward making the condition of each state secure as such but of maintaining the freedom of each within the federation so that there will be no insecurity.

This union, Kant was sure, could be extended to all states. The fruits of peace would be so great that those who did not first enter into the union would see the fruits of peace and seek entrance. Reason will prevail and put into effect the law of nations in bringing about the federation.[26]

It is interesting that Kant thought the narrower or wider community of all nations on earth has in fact progressed so far that a violation of law and right in one place is felt in all others. Hence the idea of cosmopolitan or world law is not a fantastic and utopian way of looking at law, but a necessary completion of the unwritten code of constitutional and international law to make it a public law of mankind. Only under this condition can we flatter ourselves that we are continually approaching eternal peace.[27]

Nature comes to the aid of the general will which is founded in reason. She uses man's selfishness that men give law greater force. If men will not use their reason to bring this about, nature will do it anyhow, howbeit with much inconvenience. Self-interest will seek eventually to further commerce through peace rather than war. This will be brought about because commerce will find war unprofitable.[28]

Kant suggested that practical men of affairs consult the maxims of philosophers concerning peace, if they ever intend to go to war. He is afraid the legislators will think this is belittling them, but he is concerned that the principles involved be brought out and discussed. He insists that people will discuss the maxims if given the opportunity to do so.[29]

Brunner

The Need for International Justice and Law

The cry over the world is that justice be done. Yet it is difficult to form accurate ideas as to what makes for justice. It is even more difficult, once they have been formed, to bring them into actuality.

The hope of the church is for Jesus Christ to reign over the world.

All people, the church says, should give their loyalty to Christ and let him have precedence over patriotism. The reign of Christ has no national or racial frontiers. It is the unconditional, unlimited community of all men over the whole world. Yet in the New Testament the people of God are a little flock scattered over the known world.[30] There will be terrible wars, but the hope is a new heaven and a new earth.[31] The reign of God belongs to metahistory, to the realm of eternal life. The last days of earthly history are not looked to as of perfect peace but as times of unprecedented world tumult.[32]

The state's taking to itself the monopoly of force has again and again overcome the war of all against all. Usually man goes about his work without expecting interference. Of course, there are the individual crimes that are committed each day, but the state takes care of these by taking to itself the right to punish and kill.

Unfortunately, the relative peace that we find within the borders of the various states is not found in the international order today. The very force that holds the state together has become the means of destroying international order.[33] The state that secures a genuine order within its border becomes a brutal oppressor and robber with respect to the outside world. Christian duty forces the believer to face facts with realism. The conduct of states is not very different from individuals and the way they behave in a weak state. There is little difference between peaceful and warlike states when it comes to seeking each his own wealth and benefit. This egoism is rampant with rare exception and is kept within bounds only by the knowledge that wars are expensive and the outcome uncertain. The strong state has better means to camouflage its egoism, better than the less favorable states. The favorable states can appear better because they find it to their advantage to keep the status quo. Yet the state with so favorable a position must be prepared to be challenged by the less favorable states. Thus evil dominates the picture of political reality.[34] The smaller states are in somewhat the same position as the large ones; they are peaceful by resignation rather than because they are less egoistic.

Chaos and the Order of Peace

Since this is the picture of nations in the world, there will be anarchy until international peace can be developed. Wars make the gains of social justice somewhat illusory, since wars are fought in such a way as to call all civilization and all culture into question. What makes the situation worse is that all modern wars are global. Mercenary armies used to destroy certain areas, but the population as a whole was not too greatly disturbed. Oxygen and hydrogen bombs have radically changed all that.[35]

Brunner in 1932 wrote, as he doubtless would like to write today, but the world's being split into two big camps would prohibit it,

> Conflict between nations will last as long as men are sinners, that is, until the Resurrection from the dead; and to the end of time this conflict will also be waged on brutal lines. But war has ceased to be a method in this conflict; the abolition of this particular method of conflict has become the question upon which the very existence of human civilization depends.[36]

War ought to be abolished, Brunner unquestionably would still hold, but that it is a possibility might loom much further in the future than it did in 1932. Brunner knew that the struggle would not cease just because war might be abolished, but the struggle would not be so bloody. Brutality would not be banished from the international scene just because war would cease.

Brunner has written over the years in favor of international law as the right step toward international unity. He has recognized that godlessness and unrighteousness have caused the international crisis, and that only repentance and righteousness can bring peace. He has realized that something must be done for the present, since we do not have ideal conditions.

In any case, the church has always been a minority in the world, and so far as it can be foreseen, it will continue to be. Consequently, we cannot ask what the international order would be if it were Christian, but what it should be with men being what they are.

Christianity brings two insights to the situation: one, realism without falling into cynicism; two, the absolute justice of intention arising from the knowledge of the principles of justice and not as secured by doctrinaire disregard of practical possibilities.[37]

The Possibilities for Peace

So far, in his handling of the principle of international law, Brunner has differed from Kant only in the Christian rather than the rationalist emphasis. They both have agreed on ends, namely: international law and its ordering of the chaos of the international situation. They both have seen the suicidal character of war.[38]

According to Brunner, there are three possibilities for peace:

1. Peace by means of a superior, uniformly coercive force.
2. Peace by law.
3. Peace by law combined with force.

The first kind of peace is "pax Romana," the elimination of war by a power imposing uniformity. This peace was a reality for a few generations. The force of nationalism has defeated this as a possibility for our era. The creation of a state on an ideological basis is not a possibility with human sin and the various forces at work today.

As for the second possibility, the rule by law took place in some measure in the Middle Ages. There was the "corpus Christianum" which provided a basis for a certain loyalty to treaties. This provided a certain unity born of the universality of Christendom. Principles and agreements of international law represented a relationship and obligation which was certainly relative, but not yet ineffective, and which set effective limits to "Machiavellian" politics. This awareness of international law could only remain in force so long as there was a certain clear Christian conviction to unite mankind and its rulers. The Machiavellian approach was certainly in some sense before Machiavelli, but support and cynical expression of the doctrine did not come to acceptability until the Renaissance with its disbelief.[39]

"Pacta sunt servanda" was not a doctrine that politicians had to deal with until the Renaissance. In spite of the political disunions, a certain spiritual unity formed a powerful counterbalance to the egoism of the power of individual states.

The cynicism and disbelief that came as a result of positivism brought anarchy. There was no longer any determined right but only the selfish calculations of power politics and reasons of state.

This must have become apparent to every one when so solemnly declared a treaty as the Kellogg Peace Pact to bar war was called "a scrap of paper." The last vestige of the supre-state union was gone. Instead of deterring war, the Pact actually accelerated war, since those who signed it had no idea of keeping it. With the coming of the totalitarian states, the abnegation of all moral principles was seen, and it gradually became clear to everyone that this group would not stop at moral scruples, for they indeed had none.

Treaties were easier to hold to in the days of more stable conditions. It is equally true that to insist on holding to a treaty after the conditions of the treaty have changed would be wrong. Injury would result instead of justice. What makes this more true is that at times treaties are forced upon nations, although they appear to be by free consent. Conditions may change for the nation forced into the treaty.[40]

The third possibility—law with force—is with federalism. States surrender their power to the federal power. The nations, however, would not give up their power when Woodrow Wilson tried to form the League of Nations. Brunner is not quite so optimistic as Kant was about the possibilities of federalism solving the problems of the world. He knew that the riddle of man is magnified into the riddle of the state and of world government.[41]

There still has to be the will to peace and the intention of peace, but unfortunately this does not come with intelligence alone, as Brunner knew so much better than Kant. Yet somehow this will to peace must be found. The great powers will have to forego the use of their power if there is to be peace.[42]

The Problem of Giving to Each What Belongs to It as a Nation

As Brunner saw the situation of the world in his writings after World War II, the hope of the world lies in international law, yet one is justified in asking if it really exists at all in any binding sense.[43]

Yet the problem of rendering to each nation its due is pressing. Each nation has a right to its freedom, and if it has not achieved its freedom, the right to self-determination. Yet Brunner noted, union born of history is more important than the intention born of the moment.

Economic well-being has to be considered. The size is not so important as the ability to create the necessary political form. Every nation which has the necessary form and has proved its ability to "make a go of it" has the right to do so. Only an international organization which can guarantee that right can claim to be relatively just. There will naturally be a question as to whether this right is unlimited. The solution of allowing the territory that it now inhabits with its natural boundaries generally might be the best solution.[44] Defense will be a factor in permitting a new nation to be set up. The necessary wealth to carry on is another important factor. The international organization should organize and supervise these arrangements according to Brunner.

Imperialism of either great or small states can be a danger to peace. The kind of government a nation adopts tells something about its possibilities. Dictatorships, for instance, are usually warlike.[45]

The classification of the rights and duties of each individual nation to a just order of the whole presupposes at any rate moral limitation of the sovereignty of the individual states. The two world wars showed the solidarity of the nations. It certainly pointed to their inseparable destiny. No nation, even as no individual, can live alone.

Federalism on a World Scale

In Brunner's thinking, it should be evident that securing justice in a supre-national state is indispensable. Yet with the great powers as they are, a moral limitation and a policy of neighborliness is essential. National states must also be preserved in the economic sphere. Statesmen have to be careful to follow the right criterion of justice.[46]

Only what is just creates lasting peace. For in the name of peace, justice must become a reality. Justice must be to assure peace. "Power in the service of justice is the watchword which issues unequivocally from Christian insight."[47]

The just sharing of power helps establish international order. It is urgent that as many nations as possible help share in this international order. The great powers have the power, but it is most important that they listen to the smaller states in their complaints. The larger powers have a conflict of interest with the smaller powers, but the conflict between the great powers makes it necessary that they court the smaller powers.[48]

To secure peace, economics, so far as possible, must be detached from the national states and controlled by supre-organization. This has been somewhat the case with the BENELUX countries, and other attempts are being made to accomplish this very thing.

Another area above national boundaries is culture. Culture is more in individual nations and ethnic groups, but still there is a real sense in which it is internationally grounded and universal in spirit. The church, which was universal so far as the West was concerned, furnished the culture during the medieval period and may do it again.[49] This hope, Brunner noted, perhaps with tongue in cheek, belongs to "the resurrection of the dead."

> It may be that the realization of the incomparable horror of modern war will compel the nations and states to devise forms of political organization which will exclude this suicidal way of settling disputes. If the idea of eternal peace within historical time is Utopia, it would be false pessimism to deny the possibility of overcoming what is called war today...We must bear in mind that even if we succeeded

> in eliminating the war of weapons, we should not have the slightest guarantee of the realization of the earthly paradise...There will still remain the task of economic justice...The protection of right by might will never be unnecessary as long as there are men who do not submit of their own free will to the judgement of right—that means as long as there is evil in the world.[50]

In the above paragraph, Brunner took note of Kant's hope for peace within history and affirms the hope that war may be banished from the face of the earth.[51]

In the realm of the state Niebuhr is more consistently optimistic than Brunner, though a pessimist by comparison with Kant because of his Christian realism. He had reminded us in relation to the state, "Man's capacity for justice makes democracy possible; but man's inclination to injustice makes democracy necessary."[52] He went on to remind his readers that the pessimists have in the past invested the ruler with absolute power for the purpose of keeping order and unity in the community. This pessimism is not consistent, for it is not made to apply to the ruler. If the ruler is inclined to deal unjustly with his subjects, the possession of power aggravates this inclination.

It would not be true to say that Niebuhr has a certain consistency which he has not modified when it comes to the international order, but the pessimism that led to liberalism in the order of the state becomes a force for the status quo when applied to the international order. It is true that Niebuhr has held a course of consistent Christian realism; for instance, he accepts the United Nations as meeting the realities of the situation. Yet he has never accepted the principle of world government. "For there is not one center of power and community in the world, great and good enough to superimpose the first pattern of unity upon the diverse and competing national forces."[53]

His emphasis seems to be on harnessing self-interest for the common good. What is good for the nations is good for us.[54] He believes that a giving to strengthen the free world was possible for governments which have it, but a sharing of wealth would be too much strain on self-interest.[55]

Summary

In summary it may be said that Kant shows amazing vision and hope, so much so that one could almost take what he has written to have been composed in our own day. Men have always admired the hope that Kant set forth in his political writings. Yet it would have to be admitted that the inscription of the Dutch inn-keeper "To Eternal Peace" with a picture of a graveyard on the signboard has been the real picture in our time.[56] But it would be wrong to say that this is the only truth, for progress has been made. At least today we have the United Nations which has averted what seemed certain to turn into full-scale wars.

It may be that John Bennett is right in saying that the United Nations is the best that man can hope for at this stage of history.[57] He feels that the veto in the Security Council is a reflection of the real situation in the world today. He believes that to ask the nations to give up their sovereignty at the present state of events is to ask the impossible. If the veto were given up, it would only lead to dividing one part of the world against the other and would hastily lead to war.[58] Brunner feels that a federal structure should be the aim of mankind. He notes that a monolithic structure of world government without a federal structure with a strict division of power would become a monster power of totalitarian character. A federal structure, he thinks, would involve a certain risk for world peace, but the risk would be justified by the chance for success. However, Brunner admits that there is no very real chance of getting such a federated world structure in the visible future.[59]

It is interesting that Kant thought a federal structure with the division of power should be the approach to the world government. He meant more of a division into executive, legislative, and judicial. He favored a congress of nations, a federal world government.[60]

Kant believed in the power of reason to bring about order and eventually world government in the world. What reason could not immediately accomplish nature eventually would. In one place he allowed for "Providence" as a "general founding, governing, and directing power," but he thought the concept ought not to be applied to specific events, for this would be illogical.[61]

Brunner believes in love and reverence for the divine law that has overcome the lust for power in the past and may do it again. When men believe the Gospel, they find this power of God as the genuinely new factor in political life.[62]

Endnotes

1. The television program took place on December 20, 1959, with Arthur Larson, an Arab whose name I did not get but who is on the Court of International Justice, and Senator Mundt from Wisconsin. Only Senator Mundt was against further World Court participation.
2. Brendon F. Brown, "Natural Law: The Moral Basis of Interantional Justice," *Vital Speeches*, Nov. 15, 1956, p. 335.
3. Arnold Bennett Hall, "Outline of International Law," *American Law and Procedure*, Vol. X, p. 1.
4. Ibid., p. 2.
5. Hendel, editor, *The Philosophy of Kant in Our Modern World*, p. 121.
6. Kant, *Eternal Peace*, Friedrich, editor, p. 121. There is real concern among men who do not write with a specific Christian intention in mind that it be understood that much work has to be done before a constitution can be set up for world government. Nathan Pelcovits has written that "constitution-making is the final step in establishing a regime of law and order." *Harper's Magazine*, November 1946, p. 598. Community has to precede the adoption of a constitution. Unless there is built up this community of spirit a constitution may do more harm than good, for it may demonstrate the already existing lack of harmony rather than substitute a new harmony. *Moral Principles in Action*, editor Ruth Anshen, Chapter 15 by Philip C. Jessup, "World Government and Mankind," p. 304.
7. Hendel, op. cit., p. 125, quoted from Cassirer X, 280.
8. Ibid., p. 125, quoted from Cassirer VI, 470.
9. Ibid., p. 125.
10. Ibid., p. 125.
11. Friedrich, *The Philosophy of Kant*, p. vii, "The Preface." This is a novel theory. It is almost certain that cognition, ethics, and political theory with moral import have a greater place in Kant's thought.
12. Kant, *The Philosophy of Law*, p. 214.
13. Ibid., p. 220.

14. Ibid., p. 222.
15. Ibid., pp. 222-223.
16. Kant, *Idea of Universal History*, p. 124.
17. Ibid., p. 124. Philip C. Jessup, Professor of Law at the Columbia University, writes in this vein. "The danger of war is so terrible and so acute in this atom-splitting age that we are forced to take the risk of too much rather than too little international control of sovereignty." *Moral Principles of Action*, editor Ruth Anshen, Chapter 15, Philip C. Jessup, "World Government and Mankind," p. 305.
18. Ibid., p. 125.
19. Ibid., p. 127. William Sadeler points out that Kant thought that man's side in this is to establish freedom; common legislation which approximates ideals as much as can be agreed upon at the time, should be enacted. He holds that Kant believed that political life did not of itself make men better but that it established conditions for men to be better. *Journal of Philosophy*, December 9, 1954, "Kant on International Relations," p. 853.
20. Kant, *The Idea of Universal History*, Friedrich, editor, p. 128.
21. Kant, *Eternal Peace*, Friedrich, editor, p. 437.
22. Ibid., p. 438.
23. Kant, *The Philosophy of Law*, p. 225.
24. Ibid., p. 227.
25. Ibid., p. 227.
26. Kant, *Eternal Peace*, p. 445.
27. Ibid., p. 448.
28. Ibid., p. 455.
29. Ibid., p. 456.
30. *Mark* 13:9.
31. II Peter 3:13.
32. Brunner, *Justice and the Social Order*, p. 200.
33. Ibid., p. 202. Of. Paul Tillich in writing about the democratic state and the forces which hold the individual state together notes, "Their national self-consciousness was rooted in a religious sense of destiny. National sovereignty was, for them, the realization of the divine, that is to say, democratic government. *The Religious*

Situation, p. 117. In one of Tillich's books, he sees forces at work that are breaking down some of the forces of nationalism; however, he does not see any immediate move toward internationalism. Even if one nation could become universal enough to suppress opposition without too much difficulty, he sees forces within that would be particular and divisive. These might become strong enough to disrupt the power structure and the whole process would have to start over again. Paul Tillich, *Love, Power, and Justice*, p. 106.

34. Ibid., p. 204.

35. Ibid., p. 205.

36. Brunner, *The Divine Imperative*, p. 471. Niebuhr has also seen the danger of a conflict between Russia and the United States as a war between two civilized powers with tragic consequences to both. He feels that there would be a better chance for world peace if there were ten centers of power in the world than there is with two centers—Russia and the United States. What makes the situation so much worse is the uncertainty that men are rational enough to overcome the dangers of war and solve their problems peacefully by giving and taking on a mutual basis. Neibuhr, "Our Relation to Russia," in *What the Christian Can Contribute Toward a Better World*, editor William Scarlette, p. 127 particularly.

37. Brunner, *Justice and the Social Order*, p. 202.

38. Brunner, *The Divine Imperative*, p. 473. Compare with Kant's *Idea For A Universal History*, Friedrich, editor, p. 124. The section on "The Christian and Force: The Problem of War" sounds Kantian in some of its conclusions. His approach to the anarchy of nations and the obsolescence of war are what I have in mind. These are Kantian with a difference. Brunner recognizes the egoism of nations and the corruption of reason.

39. Ibid., p. 206.

40. Ibid., p. 207.

41. Brunner, *The Divine Imperative*, p. 473.

42. Brunner, *Justice and the Social Order*, p. 208. Stringfellow Barr notes that either we have a strong international law or each nation will strive to protect itself by force by war, if necessary. Yet this is the area that law is responsible for. This is needed as a reminder

because, unlike in other areas, we are a people who have been Christian and become secularized. In other times, the problems centered around people who had not yet become Christian. Stringfellow Barr, "The Duty of a Christian in the Modern World,"*What the Christian Can Contribute Toward A Better World*, p. 183.

43. Arthur M. Schlesinger, *The Rise of Modern America*, p. 473, pointed out that there is a provision for an International Court of Justice (essentially a carry-over from the old World Court). While the court sits and solves problems, many of the major problems to date have been going to the Security Council, but the propaganda fight between the East and the West and the power struggle that has been going on does not permit much of a legal juristic nature to be accomplished there. The United States belongs to the International Court of Justice, but it adheres to the so-called self-examination clause which means she can submit to the court only such cases as she chooses.

44. Brunner, *Justice and the Social Order*, p. 215.

45. Ibid., p. 216.

46. Ibid., p. 217. It is interesting to see what a modern Christian diplomat has to say on the same subject of thr U.N. as a symbol of conscience. "The sovereign national state, to which so much reverent devotion is paid in the various gradations of patriotism and chauvinism that make up national feelings, has no foundation in Christian principle, whatever its secular justification. Nowhere in Christ's teachings was it suggested that mankind ought to be divided into political families of this nature, each a law unto itself, each recognizing no higher authority than its own national ego, each assuming its interest to be more worthy of service than any other with which it might come into conflict. Surely this whole theory is an absurdity from the Christian standpoint. Before we would achieve Christian foreign policy we would have to overcome this unlimited egotism of the sovereign national state and find a higher interest which all of us could recognize and serve." George F. Kennan, "Foreign Policy and Christian Conscience," *The Atlantic Monthly*, May 1959, pp. 46-47.

47. Brunner, *Justice and the Social Order*, p. 220.

48. Ibid., p. 220.

49. Berdyáev sees the medieval period of preserving the rights of indi-

viduals and their innate right. *The Realm of the Spirit and the Realm of Caesar*, p. 77.

50. Brunner, *Justice and the Social Order*, p. 226. Kant's words similar to Brunner's affirmation above are "Hence the idea of cosmopolitan or world law is not a fantastic and utopian way of looking at law, but a necessary completion of the unwritten code of constitutional and international law to make it a public law or mankind." Kant, *Eternal Peace*, p. 448.
51. Ibid., p. 226.
52. Niebuhr, *The Children of Light and the Children of Darkness*, p. xi.
53. Ibid., p. 173.
54. Niebuhr, *Discussion Outline and Work Paper*, p. 29.
55. Ibid., p. 34.
56. Kant, Friedrich, editor, *Eternal Peace*, p. 430, .
57. The so-called self-judging, or the Conally Amendment to the United Nations Charter dealing with the Court of International Justice bears him out. This gives those who availed themselves of the clause the right to say whether they will be judged by the Court or not. *Small World*, December 20, 1959, C.B.S. TV.
58. John Bennett, *Christianity and the State*, p. 189.
59. Brunner, *Christianity and Civilization*, Part 2, p. 123.
60. Kant, *Eternal Peace*, Friedrich, editor, p. 444.
61. Ibid., note on p. 448.
62. Brunner, *Christianity and Civilization*, Part 2, p. 125.

CHAPTER X

The Christian Idea of Justice

The Christian Affirmation

The thesis of this work is that the Christian idea of justice and law has its basis in the Christian conception of man. The basis of all earthly justice and of the legal order between men is God's order of creation. Man is a person having from God's creation his divine origin and dignity. This Biblical personalism distinguishes the Christian West from antiquity. It is true that this conception has not always been dominant, but it has always been effective as a norm and standard. Man has his rights because they have been established by God as the "birth rights of mankind" and are a part of God's order of creation.

In the Christian faith, then, this order of belonging is an order of "nature." Nature is not to be understood in a pantheistic sense, but in the sense of God's creation. In creating, God gives what he creates its own shape; he defines what belongs to its own rightness.[1]

The thesis of this work differs from that of Paul Tillich in that his is founded on ontology which in the last analysis is Greek and not Christian. He relies ultimately on the doctrine of the logos which is the basis of his ontology. Permeating the world is the logos which is reason. Every problem of knowing is ontological, and this ontology leads us to being.[2] Being leads to God, for "God is He that is being-itself."[3] It is true that love is known in its fullest in the final revelation of God, but there is also the assurance that love is known in being, and presumably in the ontological structure to some extent.[4]

"Love, power, and justice are one in the divine ground; they shall become one in human existence," Tillich writes. He is right in asserting love, power, and justice as being one in God, but Berdyáev criticizes the impersonalism of the ontological position at its weak point in favor of a personalistic approach. "Personality is outside all being. It stands in opposition to being."[5] Although Tillich is right in placing love, power, and justice in the nature of God, the Christian position is always personalistic. Niebuhr criticizes the concept of being in this way:

> Men will seek for a metaphysical validation of such a faith in vain. No degree of metaphysical speculation can ever derive the reality of historical purpose and meaning from the concept of "being." If we believe man's historical existence to be meaningful, we do so by faith and not by reason. For nothing in these structures and symbols of meaning follows in a necessary manner from an analysis of fixed structures of nature or laws of logic.[6]

The point raised, then, is that God is known to be a person as man is confronted by him. God has created his order of right which is because he exists and is known. Paul Ramsay is nearer right than Tillich in asserting that the created order is seen as law by virtue of God's faithfulness. In other words, the constancy of associating God's faithfulness in his created order is seen by analogy as law.[7]

The order of creation is made up of two parts: God who is the creator, and his creation with its God-given order. God transcends his creation; justice is immanent in this creation. Brunner sees justice as God's will for his world. He holds that God is not justice. He sees God as love.[8] This dichotomy is wrong, as justice is implicit in God's being holy and righteous.[9] This whole idea of justice and righteousness carries implicitly the idea of justice being in the very nature of God. Justice is not second-rate love, nor is it only God's will for man apart from God's own nature. The Christian doctrine of atonement, as the West has understood it, points to both justice and love being in the nature of God.[10]

Law and Ethics

The eighteenth-century "law of nature" school of jurists looked upon law and justice as purely moral ideas.[11] In the famous case of Moses v. Macferlan, Lord Mansfield brought the concepts of natural justice and equity into one section of the common law. The reason for bringing in the concept "ex aequo et bono" from the Roman law was that there was a real need for the concept in the common law to bring it to a place where greater justice could be rendered.[12] It is surprising that Thomas Jefferson at first opposed this addition to the common law and introduced a resolution into the Virginia legislature calling for the banning of "Lord Mansfield's innovations." Fortunately the resolution never passed.

As law became more technical, much of it carried no particular moral connotation, that is administrative law generally may be said to be in this category. Pound wrote,

> All the conflicts and overlappings of expectation that law must resolve are not here a mere matter of applying moral precepts. If it were, the task of the lawyer and the judge would be an easy one. It is far from true that every law or legal precept is or can be declared or applied to morals.[13]

Pound gave this case to illustrate his point. A tailor in good faith took another's cloth and made a suit of clothes. He did the tailoring thinking the cloth his own. Who owns the suit? It seems that many men of law since the time of Roman classical law have attempted to solve the problem. Every possible solution has been proposed.[14]

Although Pound's point is well taken, the case beyond a point is morally irrelevant. The man who got the suit would have to reimburse the other person, or persons, depending on who won the case in court. Pound did not mean to imply that morals have no place in law. He felt that the common law reflects the ethical stage of civilization at the time under consideration. He believed that law also receives ethics through the ideas that men pick up in reading, their conversations, and in their work together.[15] He believed, and did his part to further the achievement, that there should be an interchange of ideas between jurisprudence, ethics, economics, politics, and sociology.[16]

Pound gives this relation of morality to law and how morality has to be considered in being used by law.

> When we have a moral principle, we cannot stop at that. We have more to do than to formulate it into a legal rule. We must ask how far it has to do with things that may be governed by legal rules. We must ask how far legal machinery of rule and remedy are adapted to the claims which it recognizes and would secure. We must ask how far, if we formulate a precept in terms of our moral principles, it may be made effective in action. Even more we must consider how far it is possible to give the moral principle legal recognition and efficacy by judicial action or juristic reasoning, on the basis of the received legal materials and with the received legal techniques, without impairing the general security by upsetting the legal system as a whole.[17]

There are times when it seems as though Pound wants the legislature to take full responsibility for putting morals in the law.[18] However, there can be no law for the courts alone, because the judges legislate. The well-known aphorism of Hughes bears this out, "The law is what the courts say it is." It is true, of course, that the legislators do have the responsibility of considering the justice of a law in formulating and passing or voting it down.

Yet Pound has never been able to see so clearly as Michlem that law must be an expression of the just and right. Michlem has emphasized this particularly in relation to the common law, for he held that when the resources of Christianity cease from feeding the streams of the common law the streams dry up.[19]

On the other hand, a book like Edmond Cahn's *The Moral Decision* puts the cart before the horse, for he seeks to find moral principles in American law, but if he has discovered how they got there, he has kept the secret well.[20] Yet it is important to realize that certain presuppositions and beliefs were held by the writers of the Constitution of the United States. The Founding Fathers, for example, incorporated in the Constitution the belief in the existence of a personal and intelligent Creator of the universe, who is at the same time the Supreme Lawgiver by title of ownership over men and their property. This same conception was expressed in the second paragraph of the Declaration of Independence, which enunciated the right of Americans to form a new political state.[21]

The principles discussed thus far are important because they have life in law, custom, and religious outlook. Laws may be, and have been, declared unconstitutional because they were too vague,[22] yet it is important to remember that all laws are formulated on the basis of some principle, be it good, bad, or indifferent.[23] The principle should not make the law vague but give it specific character and much better ensure its enforcement.[24] People are obedient to laws that embody principles they really believe in and accept.

That ethics enter into law can be seen from the fact that when Christianity came into prominence in the empire, the laws gradually changed to embody Christian ideals. Northrop points to the way changes came to be made to fulfill Christian ideals. He attributes the changes to the *res gentium*. He does not mean the *res gentium* of the sociological sciences, for that only told what was true at the time. He sees rather the change as coming "from the empirically verified science and philosophy of nature."[25] Maritain tells what constituted the "empirically verified science and the philosophy of nature." He holds that the *res gentium* starts from the more profound principles of natural law and by conceptual reason and use of positive law arrives at the law of nations. "In a word, it is based upon the natural order of morality, but it emanates necessarily from this order as the first moral juridical order."[26]

When St. Patrick came to Ireland, he found the laws crude and pagan. Under his guidance and the influence of the Christian Gospel, the laws gradually were transformed. Calvinism showed a like transforming power in New England. This transforming power was so great that the Puritan influence has had a singular effect for good upon the ethical and economic outlook and output of the United States as a whole.[27]

It is true, as Stumpf has pointed out, that ideology moves into the content of the law. Stumpf further pointed out that the jurists have a responsibility to find the justice which is the basis of our justice. If they do not see the relevance of this, they have the responsibility to show some basis for showing the justice or the injustice.[28]

The Law of Nature

Although it has been tried, it has never been possible to make the Decalogue the basis of legal justice. In fact, the Old Testament laws have not been very usable, because these laws were given to the people of Israel over a thousand years ago in its specific historical situation, which was very different from our mechanized civilization.

Perhaps the naive type of Christian will be surprised to find that the line of legal development in the West has not been Biblical but has tried to make use of the "jus divinium" and brought it to bear upon the human situation by applying it with the concept of the "lex naturae." To be more exact, the divine law was identified with the ancient philosophical concept of the natural law. For fifteen centuries the divine law in its Biblical and Christian sense was the foundation of juridical thinking in Europe. The Christian ethic was the content of the natural law for the most part during this time. At the Renaissance, the rationalistic interpretation came more and more to be substituted for the Christian content.[29] Historicism and naturalistic positivism abandoned the law of nature, and legal theory no longer had a normative principle for what constituted justice. Law became a matter of mere political power and force. There was no law above the state.[30]

Kant took a different line in his thought of the state and natural law. The state was made up of individuals. The individuals gave up their freedom, which in the state of nature was wild and lawless, for order, which restored to each man his freedom undiminished. Now the individuals in the state lived in lawfulness or right. This dependence on the law is a self-legislation by each individual's own legislative will.[31]

It is the nature of the state that it be coercive, but it enforces only those laws of the reason which are in accord with the theory of duties. In ethics the will of each person enforces these laws, which are essentially the legislation of the will in accordance with the principle of universality and the categorical imperative. These duties, as they can be applied in the external world, are enforced by the coercive power of the state.

Kant's reason may be so impersonal that it abstracts from life, with the result that the content of personhood and the reality of facts are not given full force, but he does have a basis of appeal against tyranny, although he was reluctant to see it used. His belief in innate rights and his theory of duties, based on the categorical imperative, at least, as Edwin Lewis used to say, "put him on the side of the angels."[32]

Modern Thomism does not doubt but that reason promulgates to all mentally mature human minds the natural law. Reason can tell what human acts are in accord with man's true nature and what rules are not in accord with man's rational nature. Roemer of the Law School of Notre Dame has put it thus:

> Natural Law is the aggregate of those rules of action, mandatory in form, which reason itself reveals as established and promulgated by the Author of nature and imposed on all men.[33]

Human reason enables men to enact positive law in accordance with natural law. These laws are said to be declaratory of the natural law.[34]

Niebuhr, in pointing out that natural law is the part of the divine law or the eternal law which is manifested in reason, points to the "endless relativities of historical rational perspective," which are obscured. According to him, the unconditioned claim for an essentially universal reason is the basis of the remarkable degree of certainty with which Catholic moralists define "justice" and "injustice" in every possible situation.[35] The importance of natural law in Catholic thinking has become too definitive. Niebuhr, therefore, accused the Thomists of embodying the social ethics of the medieval period in its system of natural law. They elevate the prejudices of the medieval period into their system and justify these principles in specific terms because of their undue confidence in reason and their uncritical certitude as to its universality.[36]

Since Thomism is the philosophy *par excellence* of Catholicism, the criticism of Niebuhr applies to all Catholic thinkers on jurisprudence. However, Maritain, the French Catholic thinker, comes nearer than many others to the Protestant position. He sees the laws governing human conduct as based upon natural law. Natural law must express the very nature of man, and "only when the Gospel has penetrated to the very depth of human substance will natural law appear in its flower and its perfection."[37]

Yet Maritain is like other Catholics in emphasizing natural law as inclination.[38] In another place he writes,

> This means that there is, by very virtue of human nature, an order of human nature, an order or disposition which human reason can discover and according to which the human will must act in order to attune itself to the necessary ends of the human being. The unwritten law, or natural law, is nothing more than that.[39]

He sees the rights of man as based upon the idea of natural law. According to Maritain, the message of the Gospel has transformed society, that is slavery has disappeared because it became clear that men were "called upon to be the sons and heirs of God in the Kingdom of God."[40]

Doubtless the power of the Gospel has transformed society and the natural law has had its effects. Certainly medieval theory gave the people certain rights as against their rulers, even to the point of deposing them if they violated the inalienable rights bestowed by the law of God and the law of nature.[41]

Yet it is still true that the Catholic theory of the common good allows too much justification of the status quo if theory suits Catholic policy. Such a claim, for instance, was made for the Catholic acceptance of the conditions in France just prior to the French Revolution.[42]

It may be, as Brunner suggests, that Kant puts unfallen man in the place of fallen man by his emphasis on reason and will as unfallen.[43] In the sphere of natural law and legal justice, it seems that Catholic thought leaves man in somewhat the same position, except that in Catholic thought man has lost the "second story" of grace. Reason is assumed to know the natural law, which is the human side of eternal law.[44]

In view of what has been already said, it is not surprising, as John Bennett has affirmed, that Protestants hesitate to use the idea of natural law, because of the tendency to rigidity in the way it is applied.[45] Natural law does not seem to make room for the variations in the human situation nor for the dynamic flow of history. Yet even Niebuhr, who has been most critical of natural law theory, has not been able to completely deny natural law, for he is forced to see in the nature of God's creation "structures of morality."[46] Yet the strong emphasis that Catholics put on a minute understanding of natural law, which is a competitive system of law applied with rigidity in such matters as birth control, has made Protestants weary of the use of natural law at all.[47]

It is certain that the modern preoccupation with the history of law to find sanctions for the content of law in the various customs of the nations is not the answer to the problem. There is no abiding sanction in law just because law has been promulgated or enacted by the sovereign power of the state.[48] Nor should the student of Christianity and law be afraid to assert the relation of Christian theology and Christian ethics to law. The student does not need to come up with so weak a statement as did a group recently at Southern Methodist when the nearest to anything Christian they could say was, "Without religion there can be no morality; without morality there can be no law."[49]

There can be little doubt that Justice Douglas saw the situation correctly when he wrote,

> We are a religious people whose institutions presuppose a Supreme Being ... When the state encourages religious instruction or cooperates with religious authorities ... it follows the best of our traditions.

> For it then respects the religious nature of our people and accommodates the public service to their needs ... we find no constitutional requirement which makes it necessary for government to be hostile to religion and to throw its weight against efforts to widen the effective scope of religious influence.[50]

Douglas is writing about the problem of separation of church and state, but his words point up the friendly relation that has existed between church and state. He does not point to the influence of religious thought on law in the Zorach case, but he writes in another book, "When the states adopts measures protective of civil liberties, it does not confer rights. It merely confirms rights that belong to man as the son of God."[51]

Bennett has noted that many jurists have criticized the natural law for the reason that law as the positive law of the state is not superseded by natural law. This would not be necessary, in any case, in times of order, but this must have been precisely the case in the initial stages of the development of the Hanseatic League, in its reliance on natural equity and law to provide standards of justice. It must have been the same in the Mediterranean world as the cities developed trade there. It must have been the case with the nascent stages of the development of the Law Merchant in English trade. Certainly this is exactly the situation today with the Court of International Justice. Many are appealing to natural law to supply principles of international justice until enough precedents have been built up to proceed with certainty on the basis of positive law alone.[52]

Certainly we are finally brought back to the truth that justice presupposes a divine order. In creating, God gave things their own shape. God defines what belongs to the rightness of things. God has created man with a claim to this but not to that. To give to man what God has willed for him is just, but to fail to give it to him is unjust. The basis of earthly justice, of legal order between men, is God's creation of man. Some things belong to man which can be taken away from him by his fellow man; the latter is injustice. "In other words, the basis of the Christian conception of justice and law is the Christian conception of man."[53]

The Idea of Justice

The idea that justice is a perennial problem for men is demonstrated by the appearance of F. S. C. Northrop's book, *The Complexity of Legal and Ethical Experience*. The fact that he saw the need for the book and wrote it is significant. He, however, desires all legal and ethical experience to be judged by the findings of the natural and the empirically verified sciences.[54] This seems to be giving all to the natural and empirical sciences at a point where the sciences are least able to furnish a solution. He feels that the discoveries of these sciences furnish sufficient "truly international positive norms" to enable mankind to deal with the problems which have to be faced.[55]

Northrop's writings serve as a reminder of T. S. Eliot's comment that this is the first age in which the claim cannot be made that society has to be made Christian. Society has been Christian and has rejected Christianity to a great extent. Eliot points out that the idea of a Christian society is one that we can accept or reject, but if we expect to have such a society, Christianity must be treated with a great deal more intellectual respect than it has so far been treated.[56] He further feels that we are living in a period in which one political philosophy has lost its cogency for behavior, and no other satisfactory one has appeared on the scene. As a people, we still give lip service to the old, although we no longer take it seriously.[57]

The amorality of science has been revealed to us in the use the Nazis made of science and the use the Russians are making of it, toward a stronger military advantage than Americans are making of it today. Science is a method, as the Nazis and the Russians have shown. It has to be used by some political philosophy and religion for either good or bad, but it cannot itself supply the ultimate motive and purpose. One may well doubt that anyone would appeal to the teachings of science in opposing the totalitarian state. The totalitarian state leaves no basis for criticism, if God and his eternal laws are left out of the picture. Cardoza has spoken of "Those demands of religion or ethics or of the social sense of justice, whether formulated in creed or system, or immanent in the common mind." He has further emphasized that the insistence that morality and justice are not law has done great wrong, and has bred contempt and distrust of the law.[58]

Thus to omit the religious influence is to omit a really creative tradition in Anglo-Saxon life. For instance, there was the development of Christian democracy. The Cromwellian influence was a great source of impulses and convictions concerning democracy. Niebuhr has suggested that this revolution's full significance for later democracy was obscured by the Restoration. However, there was continuity with later British democratic development, in any case.[59]

Kant saw justice in terms of a society which reason by legislation could bring under order, because he saw life in terms of simple harmony. Men have but to obey the moral law, and under the coercion of government all will be well. The coercion of government will guarantee to each so much freedom and will not interfere with the freedom of others. There is the inborn right of equality before the law.

As a Christian thinker, Niebuhr has not been able to see life so harmoniously as Kant. He has pointed again and again to the tragic choices in the realm of justice. The attempts at justice in the world are colored by economic interest. Nor can justice be established in this world by purely moral suasion. It is achieved as some kind of decent equilibria of power.

Every form of justice has been achieved, in fact, by some equilibrium of power.[60] Niebuhr believes in the Christian facing the facts in the economic sphere. He is himself, although a Christian thinker, a political realist to the full:

> All political positions are morally ambiguous because in the realm of politics and economics, self-interest and power must be harnessed and beguiled rather than eliminated. In other words, forces which are morally dangerous must be used despite their peril.[61]

All these are elements in any consideration of justice. They are the stuff out of which any national economy is made. There is danger in pessimism, but perhaps much more danger in the sentimentalism of the less theologically grounded Social Gospel thinkers.[62]

Yet there can be little doubt that many of the Social Gospel thinkers, like Washington Gladden and Walter Rauschenbusch, grasped something of the radical demand of giving to each his due in fairness and equity.[63] Justice requires that a right relation be kept between property and persons. As Locke saw so clearly, property is important to individuals and society. He thought governments were instituted "for the mutual preservation of their lives, liberties, and estates."[64] There can be no doubt that Locke saw property as liberating the owner of it. He did not foresee that it might lead to the enslavement of its owner or others.[65] It was his aim and desire to harmonize the findings of seventeenth-century science with the Christian religion.[66]

Yet the wisdom of one generation may be a detriment to another. Property during the latter half of the nineteenth and the early part of the twentieth century led to what Brandeis has termed "industrial absolutism." What he meant was that property came to be used strictly for the owners without any regard for the workers. He saw that "either political liberty will be extinguished or industrial liberty must be restored."[67] Woodrow Wilson with his strong Calvinistic background expressed the proper relation of property to persons when he wrote, "What I am interested in is having the government of the United States more concerned about human rights than about property rights. Property is an instrument of humanity; humanity isn't an instrument of property." He saw law as coming to the assistance of the individual. "It must come to his assistance to see that he gets fair play; that is all but that is much ... Freedom today is something more than being let alone."[68]

Justice and the State

There is fairly unanimous feeling today that there will never be a totally Christian society. The Christian can only work for a Christian organization of society. Eliot is right when he holds that the state will never be a Christian state, only negatively Christian. The state will be under the necessity of respecting Christian principles. Still the state can be a reflection of the Christian society which it governs.[69]

Whether in the state or in communal living in the family or in the local village, there is a feeling among the common people that justice is a possibility. Laws, these citizens feel, ought to give effect to the truth and the right, and all will be well. Although the Bible did not serve as the basis for law as much as the common citizen assumes, there is still the feeling, and rightly so, that Biblical ideas do permeate the structures of justice and guarantee a certain equity and rough justice.

As a matter of fact, the chancellor was appointed originally to ameliorate the harshness of some areas of the common law so that true equity could be done. The first chancellors were priests (this was in the medieval period), and the canon law and general principles of equity were to be applied. There can be no doubt that much of the early harshness of the common law was modified, by the courts of equity.[70] It must be admitted that in time the principles of equity became less flexible, and the rules were applied by a common law judge sitting in chancellory, with a different robe to symbolize the change of rules to be applied. Yet equity does give more leeway to the judge to fairly judge the case. Still it seems that equity no longer serves the creative function it once did.[71] However, with the coming of the New Deal the Courts come to render more liberal and equitable decisions, so much so that at the present time the Supreme Court of the United States is under fire for being too liberal from the right wing elements in our country.[72]

Our contention about justice is brought out in all this struggle for power and for some right. This contention is that justice is present as an immanental principle in God's order of creation. This is seen in the fact that every group in the nation and every nation claim that they are fighting, not for their own existence, but for certain values which transcend their existence. This claim need not be wholly spurious, for groups within a nation, and nations also, are in the same position: they feel the need to justify their positions of egoism by embodying some transcendent ideal. Yet no group or nation is ever as unselfish as it claims to be, nor does it ever embody the universal value or ideal so completely as it claims.[73] Still it is significant that there is the need to appeal to ideals beyond the power structure.

Perhaps it is possible to say that every state, in its attempt to embody justice, will at the time of its inception or its moment of highest idealism, be bound together by some particular religious creed. Thus James Bryce believed the United States embodied such a creed.

> There is a hearty Puritanism in the view of human nature which pervades the instrument of 1787 ... It is the work of men who believed in original sin, and were resolved to leave open for transgressors no doors which they could possibly shut. Compare this spirit with the enthusiastic optimism of the Frenchmen of 1789. It is not merely a difference of race temperaments; it is a difference of fundamental ideas.[74]

Justice is strived after in terms of the ideal that gives the nation cohesion, although, of course, this still does not completely protect a nation from thinking itself more righteous than it is, but still there is an approximation of the ideal in terms of some aspect of justice and right. With the American Constitution it was freedom under law.

John Bennett has suggested that Anglo-Saxons at the Oxford Conference on Church Community and the State in 1937 were unanimous in affirming a positive interpretation of the state's origin and function. They generally took a more optimistic view of human nature and took for granted the idea of limited state power. They saw the limited state, as they had known it, as no great threat to the freedom of society.

> The state serves the divine purpose by realizing the ideals of humanity, freedom, equality and universal well-being and by guaranteeing to all men the most favorable external condition for their self-development.[75]

It is possible that modern Americans stood previous to the Second World War more with Kant than with Brunner in this matter of human nature as it relates to man's place in the world. The optimistic view was hardly Kantian, however, since it stemmed from Rousseau. Unfallen man had to live in a society where property and institutions brought about evil. This is not to say that this outlook was the case with the Oxford Conference, for the root of hope with this group was in Christ who redeems men. However, all optimistic views of human nature were to be severely shaken in the direction of pessimism by the demonic forces let loose by Hitler's Germany and the Japanese Empire, giving rise to World War II and subsequent international tensions.

The nature of man is relevant in discussing the state. Kant saw this relation and even mentioned in several places in his political works "the evil principle" in man. Brunner has seen this relation also in pointing out that the Christian conception of justice and law belongs to the Christian conception of man. He further saw the problem in pointing to the nature of the state as power and coercion.

Man owes his duty to the state because he first owes his duty to God. The sovereignty of God is the ultimate basis for the right and duty of the person to claim for himself and his neighbors the kind of freedom the democratic constitutions protect.[76]

Both Kant and Brunner in some measure see the state in terms of compulsion and power. Theologian Karl Barth has an interesting slant on the state. He is clear about the provisional character of all that the state accomplishes; yet he sees the chief function of the state to make it possible for men to preach the Gospel.

> It (the state) serves to protect man from the invasion of chaos and therefore to give him time; time for the preaching of the Gospel; time for repentance; time for faith. Since "according to the measure of human insight and human capacity" and "under threat and exercise of force" (Barmen Thesis No. 5) provision is made in the state for the establishment of human law and (in the inevitably external, relative and provisional sense) for freedom, peace and humanity, it renders a definite service to divine Providence and plan of salvation, quite apart from the judgment and desire of its members.[77]

This is certainly an unusual approach to the state. Back of this viewpoint there is, however, a too pessimistic view of the state as only coercive. Niebuhr criticizes Brunner for his Lutheran pessimism at times, but in the matter of the state he does not seem to be too different.

> Since there can be no ethical action without self-criticism and no self-criticism without the rational capacity for self-transcendence, it is natural that national attitude can hardly approximate the ethical ... The nation is a unity held together much more by force and emotion than by mind.[78]

The "Christian" nations are those who prove themselves so because they are still receptive to prophetic words of judgment spoken against the nation.[79] The state will never be Christian in any positive sense, for if it could, it would be confused with the church or even would be symbolic of the rays of the Kingdom of God lighting the horizon. The main function of the state is the ordering of society. This is not to say that the state will be indifferent to human need and may be forced to take on such activities as running hospitals and homes for the aged. However, these are considered by the prophets as but rendering justice to those in real need. It is significant to note that almost without exception these institutions have a reputation of being poorly run. Less than justice not more than justice is the rule. This is not to say that someone with a great love in his heart does not come along with such force and power that he can bring light into the lives of all who touch upon him. No doubt such a person brings love to all whose lives touch upon him, but if he is really to do justice, he must work to see justice done to those in need; otherwise the love will be lost in a system less than just. Robert MacIver seeks to account for this aspect of the state by holding that "Coercive power is a criterion of the state but not its essence."[80] To take this view is to fail to see that the chief function is coercive power to the extent that it must keep order and secure obedience to the law. There can be no doubt that in the early days of the New Deal, particularly, the state was looked at to serve the purpose of realizing the ideals of justice and humanitarianism in its various projects for human betterment. One of the Four Freedoms enunciated by Franklin Delano Roosevelt was the freedom from want. There was a strong appeal to equality through condemnation of the "Economic Royalists." The ideal of self-improvement was held up as an ideal and furthered by the government's granting money for the development of the arts. One of the reasons for F. D. Roosevelt's success was that people believed that through the New Deal he was giving them a "square deal."[81] The people, during the early New Deal, were not always aware of what was happening, but the government could act forthrightly because of the people's faith in the strong energetic leadership of Roosevelt. Laws were being written with equity in mind. A strong government did away with the inactivity of the latter days of the Hoover Administration. All men were equal before the law. All the citizens had to be obedient before the law.

That all the hopes of the early New Deal were realized is not claimed, but it is clear that people expect their government to use the power it possesses to administer justice with equity. The essence of the state is not coercion alone,[82] but coercion provides the climate so that order and justice may be done according to God's order of creation.

In 1954 the words "under God" were added to the Pledge of Allegiance. The addition was hailed with satisfaction by most people, for they felt that this was the expression of the true condition of our country. Although there is separation of church and state, this separation is seen as "benevolent separation." The intent is for "mutual understanding and sympathetic cooperation."[83]

The benefits of the state come from a strong state which orders society so that all men may have equality before the law. Yet it must be remembered that the state partakes of sin and is constantly tempted to embody the sin of egoism and pride in the use of power. However, when the people express in their living and the general will (in democracies) the demand for the right use of power, a state can reflect through its laws something of the concern for the people that each has his due. Of course, the equilibria of power groups can help secure justice when the various groups are of relatively equal strength. Justice in the state is not achieved until there is enough force to guarantee the restraint of egoism through the balance of power of the various groups.

The essence of the state is power,[84] but it is power to be used rightly according to the immanental principle of justice in God's order of creation. This is why the state at a particular time can reflect the idealism of a people in putting through just legislation as at the beginning of the New Deal. At another time it can see itself using its power to restore the union, while at the same time establishing a government "of the people, by the people, and for the people."[85] Lincoln was confident that God would give victory to the just. "If the Almighty Ruler of Nations, with his eternal truth and justice, be on your side of the North, or yours of the South, that truth and that justice will surely prevail by the judgment of this great tribunal of the American people."[86]

The church must exhort governments and ordinary men to found a society on justice and law. The administering of justice calls for independent, conscientious, responsible persons, to whom the task of maintaining justice and order can safely be entrusted. Justice here on earth takes its deepest meaning from the observation of God's commandments in this shattered world. The church must bear this in mind as a part of its apostolic and missionary task.[87]

Freedom and Equality

Both Kant and Brunner agree that men have an innate right to freedom. This belongs to the created order of things, Brunner held, hence liberty may be considered an integral part of the created order in which God has placed man. Men have the right to be free religiously to practice their faith, just as they have the right to their bodily freedom. An important legal freedom, Brunner pointed out, is the right of habeas corpus. In English countries it is the guarantee of personal physical freedom. The reason this looms so important in our time is that the totalitarian state sees itself as owning the human person, body and soul, whereas the divine order of creation gives man freedom so that he belongs to no man and no system. It is true that there may be limitations upon personal freedom as, for example, military service, but this is for the general good which men must consider more important than their own lives.[88]

Men have the right to property and to the expression of their sexual facilities within the bounds of Christian justice and love. These two rights have, of course, been abridged in our lifetime by Russia and Communist China. These are two of the most terrible abridgements of freedom. Property gives man a freedom of action he does not have otherwise; without the right to ownership there is no freedom. Over what he can acquire man should have freedom to exercise his will in accordance with justice.[89] The enforced practice of eugenics, regulating human procreation according to the plan of the state, is a destruction of human dignity and human personhood.

Freedom implies human equality.[90] This equality is a part of God's order of creation. When freedom was cut off from God as its guarantor and its source, mass man emerged. Men are equal before God and equally responsible to God. However, God has given to each a different function to perform which is possibly an inequality of a sort, but it still does not detract from the primal equality of men. Even Niebuhr has been brought to comment on this favorably,

> It is high time that Christian libertarians learned something of the paradoxical relation between liberty and equality in the heart of democracy. Democracy does not mean absolute equality, for no society can live without differentiation of functions which qualify equality.[91]

Love and Justice

Brunner sees the principle of justice as "to everyone his own." As the Apostle Paul put it in Romans, "Owe no man anything."[92] This principle of justice is immanental in God's created order. Justice is God's will for the world. God is above the created world; justice is his will for the created order. Justice takes, therefore, second place, never first place which is the place for love. There is always an element of the preliminary in justice. "Just as the Gospel is higher than law; love is higher than justice."

There is no dualism meant by Brunner in making this contrast. There is none because justice is a manifestation of love. Justice is that love which applies to order. It is really love as it can be realized within order or structure or institution. The origin of all orders, hence the origin of justice also, is like the origin of creation as such; it is God's love. This is why for the Christian the service of justice and its order is always a service out of love. The motive of the Christian is love, even when his action is doing justice. Justice comes from love, but it is different from love. The unity of origin does not do away with the distinction in content.

The Christian has to do justice because it is God's will for the created order. Yet he knows that justice is not an ultimate, and that doing justice is never a sufficient motive. This is the place for love. The Christian knows that the demands of love are above those of justice and that he should not only treat his neighbor as a member of an order of justice, but also, and more important, as a brother.[93]

The demands of justice end with the individual. Love is all-embracing, because it keeps its eyes on the neighbor himself rather than "something." I owe my neighbor myself and am, therefore, never done with him."[94]

Niebuhr criticizes Brunner for his too-Lutheran excluding of the rules of justice from the domain of law.[95] He points for emphasis to Brunner's statement, "If I feel that I ought to do right, it is a sign that I cannot do it ... Willing obedience is never a fruit of the sense of 'ought' but only of love. This position lacks criteria for the achievement of a relative justice."[96]

Niebuhr feels that Brunner's position interprets the doctrine of justification by faith in such a way that it leads to a complacent acceptance of injustice. He points to Brunner's teaching about the judge and the way he must administer the law as it is, strictly to the letter. "The judge must deliver his sentence in accordance to the law in its present state, even though he may be personally convinced that the law is unjust ... He knows he cannot create a better law and in this world law is necessary; but he also knows that so long as the people who frame the laws are unjust ... there will be no truly just system."[97]

Niebuhr's own position lays stress on the inherent ambiguities of social existence. He lays stress on the need for the translation of love into a real but precarious justice. This justice must be directed to the necessary limitations of social and economic life and responsive to its ever-changing conditions.

> Sacrificial love is clearly not a simple possibility as either secularized Christianity or modern liberalism assumes. It is nevertheless necessary to preserve the ultimate norms as exemplified in the "love of Christ" for the moral life of man, not as a simple possibility, not as liberal Christianity would have it ... but as symbol of the indeterminate possibilities of love in which human freedom stands.[98]

Niebuhr emphasizes that love does not propose abstract schemes of justice that leave the human factor out of account.[99] Nor can there be any attempt to substitute the law of love for the spirit of justice. For love is the fulfillment and the highest form of the spirit of justice. The attempt to substitute love for justice comes from the failure to measure the power and persistence of self-interest. It must be recognized that self-interest is not easily overcome, even in the life of the "redeemed," and that most of "the harmonies of life are not the perfect harmonies of fully coordinated wills but the tolerable harmonies of balanced interests and mutually recognized claims."[100]

It is interesting that De Wolf levels the same criticism at Niebuhr that Niebuhr has leveled at Brunner. He feels that Niebuhr has no principles to guide decision in regard to social problems. He points to the lack of connection he feels exists between Niebuhr's political decisions and his Christian theology. To illustrate his belief, he points to Niebuhr's defense of the aggressive attack by Israel, France, and Great Britain upon Egypt. He thinks Niebuhr is caught in a dilemma he has accused Barth of, namely, "There is no moral answer to our moral dilemma" though "there is a religious answer." De Wolf believes that Niebuhr draws his political direction from sources other than those presented in the structure of his present theology. He asserts that the real source of these may be in his American patriotism, his long identification with the liberal wing of the Democratic Party, and vestiges of political thinking developed in the days when he was a liberal.[101]

De Wolf's own answer is to allow the need for justice in the world where love cannot solve the present problems. However, love and justice are really one. He says, "Justice is a right ordering of love's expression." He sees love as setting the goal, putting the one loving in the proper perspective, and promoting daring resourcefulness to correct the mileau out of which justice had to mete punishment. "Love is the creative, revolutionary forward edge of justice. Justice is the appropriate application of love in an imperfect and complex situation ... Christian love motivates justice at its best ... Justice is at best a *modus vivendi* of the divine with the imperfect and worldly."[102]

Brunner undoubtedly makes too much of the separateness of justice from love in the present world. His own analogy of justice to love, as being like a glass of water to its running over, is a good one and satisfactory. Brunner is too interested in exalting love and in depreciating Kant in his assertion that if a man feels that he ought to do right he cannot. He certainly is wrong in his assertion that the judge can only strictly apply the law as it is. In common law countries the judge has some real choice through the application of the better precedents and through legal reasoning. To perhaps a lesser extent, the judge in civil law countries has some leeway to decide for the more liberal interpretation of the law.

To some extent De Wolf's criticism is just. Niebuhr sometimes speaks of justice as "second-rate love." This tends to disparage the place of justice in the order of creation. It is dangerous to speak of a "law of love" for this tends to an abstraction of love, since it is the nature of love to be free and personal. This may be why Niebuhr finds it hard to see the relevance of love in such a concrete situation as the

Pineville incident.[103] One might speak of the relevance and the irrelevance of love.

Yet, it is hard to see that De Wolf has done more than say that justice is a proximate love, the best achievable in a particular situation.

Although one might question such areas of Tillich's thought as his use of ontology and symbolism, he does make a significant contribution when it comes to setting for the relation of justice to love. He has a formal analogy but a fine one. "But we speak for a love in which justice is the form and structure of love...Love makes justice just."[104] Love and justice in his thought have ontological grounding. "They precede everything that is. They have ontological dignity."[105] One may question whether they have their source in God. There is an analogy of personhood rather than of being. The relation is one of will and faith rather than of ontology.[106]

Justice by its nature has to be reduced to rationality while love is always filled with mystery. The atonement of our Lord throws light upon the problem at this point, namely, that love must satisfy justice to be real love.[107]

No doubt, then, love has to be the content of justice, if the relation of form and structure to content is carried through. If the content of God's will is justice, then certainly justice must be in the nature of God.[108] Justice has to be taken more seriously than those thinkers who see it only as God's will for the present world or a *modus vivendi* of the imperfect and the worldly. Of course, justice has its work in the realm of systems where the situation is on what is due, rather than on the personal where love can flow freely. A person can, for instance, make his personal witness in the industrial field, but it has to be on the basis of personal integrity and influence. If his witness of love is in his managerial decisions less than justice, his love is seen as a cover for hostility.[109] The self-righteousness of such love is an engine of evil in the world. Every person must get his due before he can live in an "agapointic way" in the family, the community, and society.

Niebuhr speaks rightly when he reminds us:

> The social ideal of Jesus is as perfect and as impossible of attainment as his personal ideal ... Whatever justice men may attain in the society in which they live, it is always an imperfect justice.[110]
>
> We cannot contemplate our political life decently without a proper and grateful understanding of the "grace of God." For the grace of

> God is on the one hand providential working in history by which God makes the wrath of men to praise him, and transmutes good out of evil.[111]

SUMMARY

The basis of the Christian conception of justice and law is the Christian conception of man. When the Declaration of Independence states that "all men are created equal," this is based on the Christian conception of man. Without this conception of man, there would be no such theory. The basis of all legal justice is God's creation of man. It is important to see also that this Creator who made man in his image be seen as the God who revealed himself in Jesus Christ. This *image dei* gives man his personhood and distinguishes the Christian from other evaluations of man. The law and the state in the Christian West have seen man with innate rights, because he belongs to God's creation. This conception differs from the totalitarian conception of man which sees all rights as belonging to the state. The state may give and take away at its pleasure. In Christian thought human rights precede the state in the order of dignity.

Justice is immanent in God's created order. It is God's will for the world because God is just and holy. God could not will justice if he were not also just. Put in another and more formal way, justice is in the very nature of God, but seen from the human point of view justice is the structure for love. Justice and love both have their ground in God's own person. Humanly speaking, justice is found in the realm of systems, whereas love influences and transforms man on the personal level. Justice is the giving to each his due, but this is furthered by the equilibria of power units in the state.

Kant saw the need for responsibility, for freedom and equality. His thought does as much as human thought can do without faith. Schweitzer says that Kant went so far as to defend the dignity of ethics that he "pretended" that utility ought not to be taken into consideration.[112] Man must obey the categorical imperative to be able to belong to the spiritual world. The state enacts as much of the demands of the categorical imperative as may be practical and applicable according to reason.

The state, according to Kant, is the result of the social contract, and should seek to carry out the general will and respect man's innate rights. However, if it does not do so, the citizen is to obey until the sovereign has a change of heart, or the publicity of the philosophers can change the sovereign. The trouble with this position is that it is too abstract and leaves out what the Christian living in God's order of creation does not leave out, namely the divine command. However, lacking this command there is still the common grace which enables man to carry on the work of the state with justice. Even though this grade is universal, or common grace, it is still grace. Response to God's command carries with it the assurance that all man owes to God is love, and when in love he has done all he can, he is justified by faith.

The chief function of the state is coercion. This is not to say that the state, having established order, will not perform other functions in response to the general will. The national government under F. D. Roosevelt was moved by idealism but also by the need to readjust the economy to new and strong forces within the state to champion the cause of the common man against the economic royalists. Without strength and confidence the idealism would have gone for naught.

The hope of man is for peace. On this point Kant and Brunner are at one. They both see the need for a federal structure for world government. Brunner goes further than Kant in anticipating that the end of war would not end the struggles in the world, but men would be left free to use their resources for good rather than destruction, for growth rather than for creating chaos. However, without a federal structure and a realization of the place of God and his created order in the lives of men, world government would be the most terrible tyranny. Buttrick has seen the possibilities under God to escape the tyranny into a real peace.

> A universal Man is a *sine qua non*, in world government for an instance; for, though world government must come in some form if our world is to remain, it can never come unless at its heart there is more than a cold scheme of government. For man must love before he can be loyal. Thus only a universal Man can win real unity in our world. Let the reader follow the implications of the universality of Jesus: He will thus explore a new Canaan.[113]

This is the hope of man, but only God knows whether this can be a real achievement for our world, or whether it points to the resurrection of the dead.

ENDNOTES

1. Brunner, *Christianity and Civilization*, Part 2, pp. 109-110.
2. Tillich, *Systematic Theology*, Vol. 1, p. 71.
3. Tillich, *Love, Power, and Justice*, p. 107
4. Tillich, op. cit., p. 280.
5. Nicholas Berdyaev, *Slavery and Freedom*, p. 80.
6. Niebuhr, *Pious and Secular America*, p. 134
7. Paul Ramsay, "Elements of a Biblical Theory," *Journal of Religion*, Vol. 29-30, October 1949, p. 259.
8. Brunner, *Christianity and Civilization*, Part 1, p. 116.
9. Leviticus 19:2.
10. Tillich, *Love, Power, and Justice*, p. 15.
11. Pound, *Justice According to Law*, p. 6.
12. Walter Wheeler Cook, "Quasi Contracts." *American Law and Procedure*, Vol. I, p. 165.
13. Pound, *Justice According to Law*, p. 7. Doubtless Pound is right so far as he goes. However, there is another dimension to this problem where the ethical ideal has embodiment in persons. Arch M. Cantrall of West Virginia Bar has pointed out that the judge is judge for twenty-four hours a day and the "personal embodiment of our American ideal of justice ... The ideal of justice seems to be innate in every American, and part of his nature is to want to look up to, and respect, his court and his judge." "The Judge as Leader: The Embodiment of the Ideal of Justice," *American Bar Association Journal*, April 1959, p. 339.
14. Pound, *Justice According to Law*, p. 7.
15. Sayre, *The Life of Roscoe Pound*, p. 353.
16. Pound, *Justice According to Law*, p. 115.
17. Pound, *Law and Morals*, pp. 66-67. The problem Pound raises is a real one for the courts. Morals can be the whipping boy for legal analysts when actually the doctrine of stare decisis may be held too strictly by the judges. Of course, the judge is not to read his own private moral concepts into the law. Walter F. Murphy points

out the instance of the pre-Roosevelt Court Packing days. "The basic approach to constitutional questions of Van Devanter, Southerland, Butler and McReynolds seemed to run along these lines: Our economic theory is that of rational good will. The Framers were also rational men of good will. Therefore, they just have intended to put into the Constitution economic theory similar to ours." "The Constitution: Interpretation and Intent," *American Bar Association Journal*, June 1959, p. 593.

18. Pound, *Law and Morals*, p. 47.

19. Michlem, *Law and Ethics*, p. 52.

20. In reviewing *The Moral Decision* in *The Christian Scholar*, William Stringfellow points out that almighty God is the source of morality and justice, and if this is true, as the Christian knows it is, *The Moral Decision* sets forth "blasphemous immoral doctrine." *The Christian Scholar*, Vol. XI, No. 3, September 1957, p. 247.

21. William Francis Roemer, "Jurisprudence and Legal Institutions," Lecture 51, *American Law and Procedure*, p. 10.

22. Allan Nevins, *Times of Trial*, p. 248.

23. Apparently the Danes of the thirteenth century must have felt this way in writing these words into their legal code. "A land shall be built by law ... so that the righteous and peaceful men may enjoy their rights and peace. The coercive power of any government is governed by law and gives to righteous and peaceful men their rights."

24. "Law, Equity, and a Man to Hear Complaints," *Life*, February 22, 1960.

25. F. S. C. Northrop, "Criticism of Ethical and Legal Norms," editor Ruth Anshen, *Moral Principles in Action*, p. 128. Albert Schweitzer sizes up the situation of the relation of ethics to law this way. "Under the influence of Christianity, philosophy's ethics acquired an enthusiasm that it had not possessed earlier. Under the influence of philosophy, Christian ethics, on the other hand, started reflecting upon what it owed itself and upon what it should accomplish in this world. Thus was born a spirit which did not allow the ethics of love any longer to tolerate injustice, cruelties, and superstitions. Torture was abolished, the scourge of the

witchcraft trials ceased. Inhuman laws gave way to others more human. A reform without precedent in the previous history of humanity had begun and was accomplished in the first enthusiasm of the discovery that the principle of love is also taught by reason." "The Evolution of Ethics," *The Atlantic Monthly*, November 1950.

26. Jacques Maritain, "Natural Law and Moral Law," in *Moral Principles in Action*, Ruth Anshen, editor, p. 75.
27. Toynbee, *A Study of Civilization*, (One Volume Edition for Volumes I-VI), p. 469.
28. Samuel E. Stumpf, "Theology and Jurisprudence" *The Christian Scholar*, Vol. XI, No. 3, September 1957.
29. The form of the law has been inherited from the Greeks and Romans and modified to meet Christian standards. The content has been infused gradually with Biblical ideas, that is the gradual disappearance of divorce in the early Middle Ages and slavery in 1865.
30. Brunner, *Christianity and Civilization*, p. 108.
31. Gierke, *Natural Law and the Theory of Society*, p. 299.
32. This was a favorite expression of Lewis in class. Edwin Lewis was for many years Professor of Theology and Philosophy of Religion at Drew Seminary. He also taught at Temple for awhile, upon his retirement from Drew.
33. Roemer, "Jurisprudence and Legal Institutions," p. 21.
34. David C. Bayne, Dean of the University of Detroit Law School has this to say of natural law. "It should be clear that natural moral law could not be other than a participation of the eternal law and a promulgation of its decrees. No man can bind himself of himself. Self-binding leaves a man free to do one's own whim ... Natural law is the order and finality of the universe." Natural law is the inclination to shun evil and do good which is found in natural reason. David C. Bayne, "The Nature of Natural Law," *The Bulletin* (The Bar Association of Erie County, N.Y.), January 1959, p. 11. Protestant thought would certainly not be so uncritical of reason and of human nature. The difference is one of degree. One cannot think of absolute differences in the consideration of natural law.

35. Niebuhr, *The Nature and Destiny of Man*, Vol. II, p. 253.
36. Niebuhr, *The Nature and Destiny of Man*, Vol. I, p. 281.
37. William Ebanstein, "Freedom," *Man and the State*, p. 20.
38. *Moral Principles in Action*, editor Ruth Anshen, Maritain's essay "Natural Law and Moral Law," p. 63.
39. Maritain, *The Rights of Man and Natural Law*, p. 71.
40. Ibid., p. 74.
41. Otto Gierke, *Political Theories of the Middle Ages*, p. 48.
42. Cairns, *Legal Philosophy from Plato to Hegel*, p. 89.
43. Brunner, *The Philosophy of Religion*, p. 76.
44. *Moral Principles in Action*, editor Ruth Anshen, "Natural Law and Moral Law" by Maritain, p. 64.
45. Bennett, *Christianity and the State*, p. 98.
46. Niebuhr, *The Nature and Destiny of Man*, Vol. II, p. 254.
47. Bennett, op. cit., p. 98. William Stringfellow, for instance, believes that the concept should be abandoned. "The Christian Lawyer as a Churchman," *The Christian Scholar*, Vol. IX, No. 3, September 1957.
48. Bennett, *Christianity and the State*, p. 99.
49. *Religion, Morality, and the Law*, editor Arthur L. Harding, Review by William Stringfellow, *The Christian Scholar*, Vol IX, No. 3, September 1957.
50. Merrimon Cunninggim, *Freedom's Holy Light*, quotation from the Zorach v. Clouson case, p. 145.
51. William O. Douglas, *An Almanac of Liberty*, p. 5.
52. Brendon F. Brown, "Natural Law: Moral Basis of International Justice," *Vital Speeches*, November 1956, p. 335.
53. Huntington Cairns, "The Law as Labyrinth," a review of F. S. C. Northrop's *The Complexity of Legal and Ethical Experience, New York Times Book Review*, December 6, 1959.
54. Ibid.
55. *Moral Principles in Action*, Ruth Anshen editor, "Criticism of Universal Ethical and Legal Norms," p. 139.

56. T. S. Eliot, *The Idea of a Christian Society*, p. 4.
57. Ibid., p. 29.
58. Cardoza, *The Growth of the Judicial Process*, p. 72.
59. Bennett, *Christianity and the State*, p. 57.
60. *Love and Justice*, W. D. Robinson, editor, collected essays of Niebuhr on various subjects written over the years, p. 300.
61. Ibid., p. 59.
62. Howard A. Slaatte, "Social Ethics," *The New Christian Advocate*, p. 27. Slaatte pleads for a recovery of the Kerygma with social implications to counteract a "social passion" without theological responsibility.
63. Niebuhr, speech reported in *Christianity Today*, Vol. II, February 29, 1956.
64. William Ebenstein, *Man and the State*, p. 327.
65. John Locke, *Of Civil Government*, p. 25.
66. Russell Kirk, "Introduction" to Locke's *Of Civil Government*, p. ix.
67. Louis D. Brandies, "Industrial Absolutism versus Political Liberty," in *Man and the State*, Ebenstein, editor, p. 506.
68. Woodrow Wilson, "The New Freedom," chapter on "Property Rights and Human Rights," in the anthology, *Man and the State*, Ebenstein, editor, p. 507. R. L. Bruckberger paints this idealistic picture of today's business and industry, "Business no longer revolves around money; money is only one of the planets revolving around business; business itself exists to serve mankind, just as medicine exists to serve mankind ... It is being conceded that the labor of a human being is not a commodity. The worker no longer sells his labor but enters into an association with management, so that what they produce together will provide a livelihood for both, and, at the same, better service for the customer. "The Great twentieth Century Revolution," *The Reader's Digest*, October 1959, p. 39.
69. T. S. Eliot, *The Idea of a Christian Society*, p. 44. It is interesting that Calvin, according to Troeltech, who is so often thought of as pessimistic, held that "The state ... is never regarded as a mere antidote to the fallen state and a penalty of evil, but it is always

chiefly regarded as a good and holy institution appointed by God Himself." Ernest Troeltsch, *The Social Teaching of the Christian Church*, Vol. 2, p. 613. Barth, *Against the Stream*, pp. 22-25. Barth has this to say in relation to the state and the Gospel, "It [the Church] proclaims the rule of Jesus Christ and the hope for the Kingdom of God. This is not the task of the civil community; it has no message to deliver; it is dependent on a message being delivered to it ... It [the State] depends on the existence of seeing eyes elsewhere. It cannot call the human Hybria into question fundamentally ... in this respect too it depends on ultimate insights existing elsewhere."

70. Walter Wheeler Cook, "Equity Jurisdiction," Vol. VI, *American Law and Procedure*, p. 143.

71. Henry Steele Commager, *The American Mind*, p. 372.

72. The weekly *Christian Economics* has consistently criticized the Warren Court for its too liberal interpretations. Their aim now is to get the so-called Right to Work Laws accepted. See *Christian Economics*, January 12, 1960, also February 9, 1960. Richard H. Mille of the Illinois Bar gives the present state of the law thus, "However, the state right-to-work statutes are in full force and effect, except to the extent that Congress has legitimately pre-empted the field." "Right to Work vs. Union Shop," *American Bar Association Journal*, June 1959, 713. One cannot help but note the extreme to the right position of *Christian Economics*. The magazine is free to ministers, and many men take the position of the magazine to be the Christian position.

73. Niebuhr, *Christianity and Power Politics*, p. 108.

74. James Bryce, *The American Commonwealth*, Part 1, p. 299.

75. *Oxford Conference, Official Reports*, quoted by John Bennett, *Christianity and the State*, p. 240.

76. Bennett, *Christianity and the State*, p. 153.

77. As cited by Karl Barth, *Against the Stream*, p. 21. Barth also sees the church present wherever there is law and order brought forth by the state enforcing its laws. On the other hand the church makes its own contribution. "The Church always stands for the constitutional State, for the maximum validity and application of that twofold rule (no exemption from the full protection by the

law) and therefore it will always be against any degeneration of the constitutional State into tyranny or anarchy ... In its politics it will always be urging the civil community to treat this fundamental purpose of its existence with the utmost seriousness; the limiting and preserving of man by the quest for and the establishment of law." Karl Barth, *Against the Stream*, p. 36.

78. Niebuhr, *Moral Man and Immoral Society*, p. 88.

79. Niebuhr, *The Nature and Destiny of Man*, p. 219.

80. Robert MacIver, *The Modern State*, p. 213. MacIver does see the state as coercive to the extent that other groups may have laws which do not have to be obeyed. All one has to do is to withdraw from the organization. It is not so with the state. One must obey its laws. Law differs from ethics also in that ethics is binding upon the conscience, but law is binding upon the actions of all. Of course these prescribed actions are external. A man cannot be punished for what he thinks. p. 157.

81. Arthur Schlesinger, "Prologue: The First Hundred Days," in *The Coming of the New Deal*.

82. Schlesinger wrote of the prideful aspect of the New Deal. "They often were irritating, but they were alive. 'The filial Aurorae make me actively sick at my stomach,' Judge Learned Hand said early in 1934; 'They are so conceited, so insensitive, so arrogant.'" *The Coming of the New Deal*, p. 17. Judge Hand was not one of the reactionary judges speaking, but one of the most respected judges in the country, and certainly one of the most learned and able.

83. Anson Phelps Stokes, *Church and State in the United States*, p. 47.

84. Brunner in his latest book, *The Letter to the Romans*, is more pessimistic, or makes his pessimism more explicit in this statement, "The possessors of political power are instruments of the divine wrath to which we ought to give place. That is the dignity, that is also the limit of the state." p. 100. Otherwise there is the same relation between justice and love and the same subordination of justice to love. "Love is greater than Justice; it does more than justice demands. The demands of justice and with the individual; love alone is all-embracing because it does not keep its eye on 'something' that one over the other but on the other himself and

myself." p. 111. It is interesting that Neibuhr, De Wolf, and Brunner, while differing on just about everything else agree in not ascribing justice to God's nature. Brunner holds that justice is God's will for the world, Niebuhr that justice is "second-rate love," and De Wolf writes, "Justice is at best *modus vivendi* of the divine with the imperfect and worldly." Harold De Wolf, *The Case for Theology in the Liberal Perspective*, p. 152. They all seem to be wrong at this point; love and justice are in the very nature of God himself.

85. Lincoln, "The Gettysburg Address," *The Pocket University*, Vol. V, Par. 1, p. 89.

86. Lincoln, "The First Inaugural Address," *The Pocket University*, Vol. V, Part 1, pp. 87-88.

87. *Man's Disorder and God's Design*, the section on "The Church and International Society," The Amsterdam Assembly Series, p. 70.

88. Brunner, *Justice and the Social Order*, p. 57. Henry R. Luce asks in a address if the West can produce a political idea. He gives his own answer, "Yes ... our idea is liberty under law." He notes that for two thousand years this idea has been elaborated in theory. There has been success in living the idea, notably in America, but the confusion has arisen in our moral breakdown and the fact that we have fallen into philosophical confusion. "The Way of Law: The Road to the Mountain of Vision," *American Bar Association Journal*, May 1959, p. 483. That Luce is right about the philosophical confusion is seen by another book, *The Definition of Law* by Herman Kantorowicz. He sees the right approach to law as that of pragmatism. Definitions are not true or false but do serve the purpose of a particular science. His definition of law is "a body of rules prescribing external conduct and considered justifiable." Review of the book by Lester Dennon, *American Bar Association Journal*, February 1939, p. 170.

89. Sir Winston Churchill has spoken nobly of freedom and the principles which make any English-speaking persons proud of their heritage of freedom. "We must never cease to proclaim, in fearless tone, the great principles of freedom and the rights of man which are the joint inheritance of the English-speaking world, and which through Magna Carta, the Bill of Rights, habeas cor-

pus, trial by jury and the English common law, find their most famous expression in the American Declaration of Independence." Quoted by Geoffrey Lawrence, Q.C., "Freedom Under Law: The Challenge to the English-Speaking Bar," *American Bar Association Journal*, December 1959, p. 1278. Lawrence's argument is that freedom is itself the answer to anarchy and not a compromise between anarchy and tyranny. Men without inheritance will use their freedom with wisdom.

90. In 1861 Lincoln wrote that the Declaration of Independence gave the promise that "the weights would be lifted from the shoulders of all men, and that all should have an equal chance." William O. Douglas quotes this in *An Almanac of Liberty*, p. 4. The Declaration is an example of how Christian ideas have worked themselves into political documents from which they find their way into law. The liberation of slaves was brought about in the Emancipation Proclamation, which was an executive order with the effect of law in wartime. The Thirteenth and Fourteenth Amendments gave freedom and a real guarantee of equality, even if the full effect is only now being felt.

91. Niebuhr, *Love and Justice*, W. D. Robinson, editor, p. 169.

92. Romans 15:8

93. Ibid., pp. 116-117.

94. Brunner, *The Letter to the Romans*, p. 111.

95. Niebuhr, *The Nature and Destiny of Man*, Vol. 2, p. 251.

96. Quoted from *The Divine Imperative*, Brunner, p. 189.

97. Quoted from *The Divine Imperative*, Brunner, pp. 253-254.

98. Niebuhr, *Pious and Secular America*, p. 141.

99. Niebuhr, *Love and Justice*, W. D. Robinson, editor, p. 154.

100. Niebuhr, *Love and Justice*, p. 26.

101. L. Harold De Wolf, *The Case for Theology in the Liberal Perspective*, p. 169.

102. Ibid., pp. 151-152.

103. Niebuhr, *Love and Justice*, p. 113.

104. Tillich, *The New Being*, p.33.

105. Tillich, *Love, Power, and Justice*, p. 21.

106. Stumpf, "Theology and Jurisprudence," *The Christian Scholar*, Vol. XI, No. 3, September 1957.

107. Tillich, *Love, Power, and Justice*, p. 14.

108. Isa. 5:16. "The Lord of host is exalted in justice."

109. Tillich, *Love, Power, and Justice*, p. 108.

110. Niebuhr, *Love and Justice*, p. 32.

111. Ibid., p. 294.

112. Albert Schweitzer, "The Evolution of Ethics," *The Atlantic Monthly*, November 1950.

113. George A. Buttrick, *So We Believe, So We Pray*.

POSTSCRIPT

Can Kant be considered an existentialist? There is much which indicates that Kant was often in a struggle. Brunner says that Kant was struggling with transcendental philosophy and Christianity. Deep down Kant did believe in God because he felt the moral universe needed a judge and ruler. Without faith in God morality in itself would be incomplete. Kant can be regarded as a precursor of Kierkegaard. Indeed the primacy of practical reason has an "existential flavor" and might be called the principle of an ethical existentialism.

One reason Kierkegaard was interested in Kant was Kant's suggestion that a moral being should be induced to believe in God as "the moral author" of nature. There is a moral need to bring together nature and ourselves as moral beings. If the moral law had no roots in the world apart from our moral consciousness, or if we as moral beings were living in a morally indifferent world, our moral striving would be entirely subjective. However, our duties are not merely subjective. They are related to the surrounding world and have an effect upon the institutions for which we work. The effect, however, is not in our hands. Although Kant's ethics exclude all considerations of our decisions and resultant actions, nevertheless we cannot help wishing that out of fulfillment moral consequences may flow. In spite of the fact that Kant does not carry out these implications of moral law, he demonstrates in a definite way the need of moral beings to believe that there is a connection between moral effort and its effect. We may call the end we pursue "happiness," not in so far as we are subject to the moral law, but in so far as we depend on the world of other beings.

How can we combine the need of happiness and the inexorable and sometimes even cruel austerity of the law? We can do this by having faith in God as creator of the world and but believing our moral needs are being met, as it were, not only in a lonely world but sensible to the moral law. If we can feel an echo beyond ourselves, the austerity of the law and the hardship of our trials can be mitigated.

In all this Kant believed that his doctrine was in complete agreement with the Christian religion although he insists that the faith which he deduces a priori from his ethical principles is purely rational." This does not make Kant an existentialist in the sense that Kierkegaard was, but does show the struggle. Kant goes more for reason as over against faith in the sense of Chalcedon, but people like Ronald M. Green in his book *Kierkegaard and Kant: The Hidden Debt* see Kierkegaard concerned with Kant's teaching and giving serious study to it.

Brunner looked at Life differently than Kant. Brunner sees Kant as a Pelagian. While Kant was strong on character, as of course Brunner would be as a Christian, Kant's emphasis was strongly ethical, "Thou shalt be a better man."[2]

Kant and Brunner seem, to have much in common, at least in part. There was a time when students thought they had to contrast Kant and Brunner or other Christians. Strangely enough there are a number of areas of thought where Brunner seems to be attracted to Kant's thought. I think a case could be made in the area of natural law. Kant wrote an essay "To Enternal Peace." Brunner also is concerned about enduring peace. He showed his concern in dealing with the Nuremberg trials. Kant and Brunner both show concern because of their knowledge of natural law and because they knew the value of peace. Brunner felt that the trials were the last occasion in modern times in which he saw natural law being seriously applied.

Interestingly enough they share an interest in radical evil. Brunner sees evil as the absence of good or lack of the divine. The presence of evil is an absence of God or an emptiness. The presence of God is the way of becoming increasingly full of the divine.

The question of evil receives by far the most serious attention where the moral will is regarded as the center of the personality and the fundamental fact in the interpretation of the world. The more purely the moral consciousness understands itself, that is, the more clearly practical reason is distinguished from theoretical reason and the theoretical interpretation of the world, the recognition of evil as a fact becomes clearer.

Kant is the only one among idealistic thinkers, indeed the only one among the philosophers of modern times, who has recognized and admitted that evil is a counter of the will to the law of good. Absolutely and clearly he states his antithesis which contradicts the false; evil is not bondage to the sensible world. It is not inertia, nor the raw material of nature, but a personal act, which takes place in the center of personality. In the reason of man, it is the self-determination of the will in opposition to the law of God. From this point of view the doctrine or "radical evil" is inevitable. Since evil is the act of the personality and cannot be exhausted in a single element, the whole personality in each of its elements is responsible for evil, and is therefore never free from evil. This is the precise meaning of "radical evil."

It should also be noted that to the definition of the good will—that nothing save a good will can be called good—there is a corresponding definition for evil. It may only be conceived as a "determined or arbitrary caprice." It is said to be divorcing the maxims from the moral law.

Kant was quite aware that it is impossible to comprehend evil, gazing at it as some fearful abyss. This led him to the conception of "inborn guilt." He reaches this conclusion because he understood what a moral will means much better than other thinkers. If the moral will is that which Kant describes in "the Metaphysic of Ethics," then he was forced to define evil as the paradox of "radical evil." We can see that both Kant and Brunner have insights which are existential.[3]

Endnotes

1. Richard Kroner, *Speculation and Revelation in Modern Philosophy*, p. 226-227.
2. Emile Brunner, *Man in Revolt*, p. 527.
3. Emile Brunner, *The Mediator*, p. 125-127

BIBLIOGRAPHY

Books

Abbagnano, Nicola. *Critical Existentialism.* Translated and edited by Nino Langiulli. Garden City: Doubleday, 1969.

Alpheus, Thomas Mason. *A Free Man's Life*. New York: The Viking Press, 1956.

Anshen, Ruth, ed. *Moral Principles in Action.* New York: Harper & Brothers, 1952.

Aquinas, Thomas. *The Political Ideas of St. Thomas Aquinas,* "Selections." Edited with an introduction by Dino Rogoniari. New York: Hefner, 1953.

Aristotle. *The Basic Works of Aristotle.* Edited with an introduction by Richard McKean. New York: Random House, 1941.

Aumann, Francis R. *The Changing American Legal System: Some*

Selected Phases. Columbus: The Ohio State University Press, 1940.

Barth, Karl. *Against the Stream,* "Shorter Post-War Writings." New York: Philosophical Library, 1954.

Bates, E. S. *American Faith.* New York: W. W. Norton, 1956.

Bennett, John. *Christianity and the State.* New York: Charles Scribner's Sons, 1959.

Berdyáev, Nicholas. *Slavery and Freedom.* New York: Charles Scribner's Sons, 1944.

———. *The Realm of the Spirit and the Realm of Caesar.* Translated by Donald A. Lowrie. New York: Harper & Brothers, 1952.

Boorstin, Daniel J. *The Mysterious Science of the Law.* Boston: Beacon Press, 1958.

Boyles, Michael D., and Kenneth Henley, eds. *Right Conduct Theories and Applications.* New York: Random House, 1983.

Brunner, H. Emil. *Christianity and Civilization.* Part 1, The Gifford Lectures, Foundations. New York: Charles Scribner's Sons, 1948.

———. *Christianity and Civilization.* Part 2, The Gifford Lectures, Specific Problems. New York: Charles Scribner's Sons, 1948.

———. *The Divine Imperative.* Translated by Olive Wyon. Philadelphia: The Westminster Press, 1947.

———. *Justice and the Social Order.* Translated by Mary Hottinger. London: The Lutterworth Press, 1949.

———. *The Letter to the Romans,* "A Commentary." Translated by H. A. Kennedy. Philadelphia: The Westminster Press, 1959.

———. *Man in Revolt.* Translated by Olive Wyon. Philadelphia: The Westminster Press, 1947.

———. *The Mediator.* Translated by Olive Wyon. Philadelphia: The Westminster Press, 1947.

———. *The Philosophy of Religion.* Translated by A. J. D. Farrar and B. L. Woolf. London: Ivor Nicholson & Watson, 1939.

Bryce, James. *The American Commonwealth.* Part 1. Chicago: Charles H. Sergels & Company, 1891.

Buchanan, Scott. *Rediscovering Natural Law.* Santa Barbara, Calif.: Center for Study of Democratic Institutions, 1962.

Buttrick, George A. *So We Believe, So We Pray.* Nashville: Abingdon-Cokesbury Press, 1951.

Cahn, Edward. *The Moral Decision, Right and Wrong in the Light of American Law.* Bloomington: University of Indiana Press, A Midland Book, 1959.

Cairns, Huntington. *Legal Philosophy from Plato to Hegel* Baltimore: Johns Hopkins Press, 1949.

Calvin, John. *The Institutes of the Christian Religion.* Translated by John Allen. Philadelphia: The Presbyterian Board of Education, 1936.

Cardoza, Julius. *The Growth of the Judicial Process.* New Haven: Yale University Press, 1924.

Carlyle, Thomas. *Heroes and Hero Worship.* London: Chapman & Hall, 1840.

Cassirer, Ernest. *Rousseau, Kant, Goethe, Two Essays.* Translated from the German by James Gutmann, Paul Oskar Krieteller, and John Hermon Randall Jr. The History of Ideas Series, no. 1. Princeton: Princeton University Press, 1947.

Commager, Henry Steele. *The American Mind.* New York: Harper & Brothers, 1954.

———. *Living Ideas in America.* New York: Harper & Brothers, 1954.

Cowan, Wayne E., ed. *What the Christian Hopes For In Society.* With a foreword by Reinhold Niebuhr. New York Association Press, 1957.

Croxall, T. H. *Glimpses and Impressions of Kierkegaard.* Digswell Place: James Nisbet, 1959.

Cunninggim, Merrimon. *Freedom's Holy Light.* New York: Harper, 1955.

DeWolf, L. Harold, *The Case for Theology in the Liberal Perspective.* Philadelphia: The Westminster Press, 1959.

Douglas, William O. *An Almanac of Liberty.* New York: Doubleday, 1959.

———. *Idea of a Christian Society.* New York: Harcourt Brace, 1949.

Dowley, Tim, ed. *Eerdman's Handbook to the History of Christianity.* Grand Rapids, MI: Eerdmans, 1977.

Ebenstein, William, ed. *Man and the State.* "Modern Political Ideas." New York: Rinehart, 1947.

Eliot, T. S. *The Idea of a Christian Society.* New York: Harcourt Brace, 1940.

Gettell, Raymond Garfield. *History of Political Thought.* New York: Appleton-Century-Crafts, 1953.

Gierke, Otto. *Natural Law and the Theory of Society, 1500 to 1800.* Volumes I and II. Translated by Ernest Barker with a lecture on natural law and humanity by Ernst Troeltsch. Boston, Beacon Hill: Beacon Press, 1957.

———. *Political Theories of the Middle Ages.* Translated with an introduction by Francis William Maitland. Boston, Beacon Hill: Beacon Press, 1958.

Halevy, Elia. *The Growth of Philosophic Radicalism.* Translated by Mary Morris with a preface by A. J. Lindsay. Boston: Beacon Press, 1955.

Hegel, G. F. W. *The Philosophy of History.* Translated by J. Sibree with a preface by Charles Hegel. New York: The Colonial Press, 1900.

———. *The Philosophy of Law. The Basic Writings of Hegel.* Edited with an introduction by Carl J. Friedrich. New York: Modern Library, 1954.

———. *Selections.* Edited by J. Loewenberg. New York: Charles Scribner's Sons, 1929.

Hendel, Charles W., ed. *The Philosophy of Kant and Our Modern World.* New York: The Liberal Arts Press, 1959.

Hobbes, Thomas. *Leviathan.* With an introduction by Michael Oakeshott. Oxford: Blackwell, 1957.

Kant, Immanuel. *Eternal Peace.* Edited by Carl J. Friedrich. Cambridge: Harvard University Press, 1948.

———. *The Metaphysics of Morals.* Translated by T. K. Abbott. London: Longmans Green, 1887.

———. *The Philosophy of Kant, Immanuel Kant's Moral and Political Writings.* Edited with an introduction by Carl J. Friedrich. New York: Modern Library, 1949.

———. *The Philosophy of Law.* Translated with an introduction by W. Hastie. Edinburgh: T. & T. Clark, 1887.

———. *Immanuel Kant 1720–1924.* Edited by E. G. Wilm. New Haven: Yale University Press, 1925. Essays by George Herbert Palmer, Mary Calking, E. C. Wilm, W. E. Hocking, Harlow

Sharpley, Roscoe Pound, and Gorhart Van Schultz, Georgetown University Press, 1925.

Knox, John. *The History of the Reformation in Scotland.* Edited by C. J. Guthrie, Q.C. (In one volume). London: Adams & Charles Black, 1899.

Kroner, Richard. *Speculation and Revelation in Modern Philosophy.* Philadelphia: Westminster Press, 1961.

Lafevre, Perry. *Philosophical Resources for Christian Thought.* Nashville: Abingdon Press, 1968.

Laski, Harold. *The State in Theory and Practice.* New York: Viking, 1947.

Lincoln, Abraham. *Selections.* Edited by Bliss Perry. *The Pocket University,* Volume V, Part 1. Garden City: Doubleday, 1925.

Locke, John. *Of Civil Government.* With an introduction by Russell Kirk. Chicago: Henry Rognery, A Gateway edition, 1955.

MacIver, Robert. *The Modern State.* New York: Oxford University Press, 1926.

Man's Disorder and God's Design. Section on "The Church and International Society." New York: Harper & Brothers, The Amsterdam Assembly Series, 1948.

Maritain, Jacques. *The Rights of Man and Natural Law.* New York: Charles Scribner's Sons, 1945.

———. "Natural Law and Moral Law." In *Moral Principles of Action,* edited by Ruth Anshen. New York: Harper & Brothers, 1952.

Mason, Alpheus. *Brandeis, A Free Man's Life.* New York: Viking, 1956.

Michalson, Carl, ed. *Christianity and the Existentialists.* New York:

Charles Scribner's Sons, 1956.

Michlem, Nathaniel. *Law and Ethics.* London: Oxford University Press, 1926.

Morgan, Edward G. *The Puritan Dilemma, The Story of John Winthrop.* Boston: Little, Brown & Company, 1958.

Nevins, Allan. *Times of Trial.* New York: Alfred A. Knopf, American Heritage, 1958.

Niebuhr, Reinhold. *The Children of Light and the Children of Darkness.* New York: Charles Scribner's Sons, 1944.

———. *Christianity and Power Politics.* New York: Charles Scribner's Sons, 1940.

———. *Christian Realism and Political Power.* New York: Charles Scribner's Sons, 1953.

———. *An Interpretation of Christian Ethics.* New York: Harper & Brothers. 1935.

———. *Love and Justice.* Edited by W. D. Robinson. Philadelphia: The Westminster Press, 1957.

———. *Moral Man and Immoral Society.* New York: Charles Scribner's Sons, 1952.

———. *The Nature and Destiny of Man.* Volume I, *Human Nature.* New York: Charles Scribner's Sons, 1945.

———. *The Nature and Destiny of Man.* Volume II, *Human Destiny.* New York: Charles Scribner's Sons, 1945.

———. *Pious and Secular America.* New York: Charles Scribner's Sons, 1958.

———. *Reflections at the End of an Era.* New York: Charles Scribner's Sons, 1954.

Peale, Norman Vincent, ed. *Faith Made Them Champions.* Carmel, NY: Guideposts, 1954.

Plato. *The Dialogues.* Translated by B. Jewett. Fourth edition. Oxford: Claredon Press, 1953.

———. *The Republic.* Translated with an introduction by A. D. Lindsay. New York: E. P. Dutton.

Pound, Roscoe. *An Introduction to the Philosophy of Law.* Revised edition. New Haven: Yale University Press, 1954.

———. *Interpretations of Legal History.* New Haven: Yale University Press, 1936.

———. *Justice According to Law.* New Haven: Yale University Press for Westminster College, 1954.

———. *Law and Morals.* The McNair Lectures 1923, delivered at the University of North Carolina. Chapel Hill, N.C.: The University of North Carolina Press, 1924.

———. *The Spirit of the Common Law.* Boston: Beacon Press, 1963.

Rommen, Heinrich A. *The Natural Law.* Translated by Thomas B. Hanley. St. Louis and London: Herder, 1948.

Ross, W. D. *Aristotle, A Complete Exposition of His Works and Thought.* New York, Meridian Books, 1959.

Rousseau, J. J. *The Social Contract.* Newly translated with an introduction by Wilmore Kendell. Chicago: Henry Rognery, 1959.

Sayre, Paul. *The Life of Roscoe Pound.* Iowa City: College of Law Committee, State University of Iowa, 1948.

Scarlette, Bishop William, ed. *What the Christian Can Contribute Toward a Better World.* Philadelphia: John C. Winston, 1946.

Schlesinger, Arthur M. *The Coming of the New Deal.* New York: Houghton Mifflin, 1956.

———. *The Rise of Modern America, 1865–1951.* New York: Macmillan, 1951.

Slaatte, Howard. *The Paradox of Existentialist Theology.* New York: Humanities Press, 1971.

Stokes, Anson Phelps. *Church and State in the United States.* New York: Harper & Brothers, 1950.

Taylor, A. E. *Plato, The Man and His Work.* New York: Humanities Press. Reprint, New York: Meridian Books, 1948.

Tillich, Paul. *Love, Power, and Justice.* New York: Oxford University Press, 1954.

———. *The New Being.* New York: Charles Scribner's Sons, 1955.

———. *The Religious Situation.* Translated by H. Richard Niebuhr. New York: Meridian Books, The Living Age Books, 1956.

———. *Systematic Theology.* Volume 1. Chicago: The University of Chicago Press, 1951.

Toynbee, Arnold. *A Study of Civilization* (One Volume Edition for Volumes I–VI). New York: Oxford University Press, 1947.

Trevelyan, G. M. *Illustrated History of England.* Revised edition. London: Longmans Green, 1938.

Troeltsch, Ernst. *The Social Teaching of the Christian Church.* Translated by Olive Wyon. Volume 2. New York: Macmillan, 1932.

Trueblood, Elton. *Declaration of Freedom.* New York: Harper & Brothers, 1955.

Watson, John. *Kant Explained.* Edinburgh: James Maclehouse, 1908.

Welch, Don. *Law and Morality.* Philadelphia: Fortress Press, 1987.

Bible References

Revised Standard Version, Thomas Nelson & Son. 1 Corinthians 7:4; Genesis 1:31, 8:17; Isaiah 5:16; Leviticus 19:2; Romans 7:6; 13:4; 15:8.

Legal Works

American Law and Procedure. Volumes I, II, III, VI, X. Chicago: LaSalle Extention University, 1953.

Articles and Speeches

Bayne, David C. "The Nature of Natural Law." *The Bulletin* (The Bar Association of Erie County, New York), January 1959, pp. 10–13.

Brown, Brendon F. "Natural Law: Moral Basis of International Justice." *Vital Speeches,* November 1956, p. 335.

Bruckberger, R. L. "The Great Twentieth-Century Revolution." *The Reader's Digest,* October 1959, p. 39.

Christian Economics, January 12, 1960, also February 9, 1960.

Cairns, Huntington. "The Law as Labyrinth," review of *The Complexity of Legal and Ethical Experience,* by F. C. S. Northrop. *New York Times Book Review,* December 6, 1959.

Cantrall, Arch M. "The Judge as Leader: The Embodiment of the Ideal of Justice." *American Bar Association Journal,* April 1959, p. 339.

Dennon, Lester. Review of *The Definition of Law,* by Herman Kantorowicz. *American Bar Association Journal,* February 1939, p. 170.

Gibbs, Nancy. "America's Holy War." *Time Magazine,* December 9, 1991.

Gordimer, Nadine. "Chief Luthuli." *The Atlantic Monthly,* April 1959.

Hennings, Jr., Thomas C. "Constitutional Law: The People's Right to Know." *American Bar Association Journal,* Volume 45, July 1959.

———. "The Supreme Court and Liberty." *American Bar Association Journal,* Volume 44, No. 3, March 1958.

Hensen, Roy D. "Law and Peace: The Problem of Generations." *American Bar Association Journal,* Volume 45, No. 10, October 1959.

Hoover, J. Edgar. "Communism: The Bitter Enemy of Religion." *Christianity Today,* Volume II, No. 19, June 22, 1959.

"Kant on International Relations." *Journal of Religion,* Volumes 29–30, October 1949.

Katz, Wilbur. " Law, Christianity and the University." *The Christian Scholar,* Volume XI, No. 3, September 1957.

Kennan, George F. "Foreign Policy and Christian Concience," *The Atlantic Monthly,* May 1959.

Kennedy, Gerald. "Could It Happen Here?" *The Christian Advocate,* February 4, 1960.

Lawrence, Q.C., Geoffrey. "Freedom Under Law: The Challenge to the English-Speaking Bar." *American Bar Association Journal,* Volume 43, No. 12, December 1959, p. 1278.

Lewis, C. S. "Screwtape Proposes a Toast." *Adventures of the Mind,* No. 42, *The Saturday Evening Post,* December 19, 1959.

"Law, Equality, and a Man to Hear Complaints." *Life,* February 22, 1960.

Luce, Henry R. "The Way of Law: The Road to the Mountain of Vision." *American Bar Association Journal,* May 1959, p. 483.

Meicklejohn, J. George. "Kantian Formalism and Civil Liberties." *Journal of Philosophy,* Volume 51, December 9, 1954.

Mille, Richard H. "Right to Work vs. Union Shop." *American Bar Association Journal,* June 1959, p. 593.

Murphy, Walter F. "The Constitution: Interpretation and Intent." *American Bar Association Journal,* June 1959.

Niebuhr, Reinhold. "Our Moral and Spiritual Resources for International Cooperation." *Discussion Outline and Work Paper,* February 1956.

———. Speeches reported in *Christianity Today,* Volume II, February 1956.

Ottonburg, Lois. "One Hundred and Seventy Years Ago: The Birth of the American Republic." *American Bar Association Journal,* Volume 45, No. 4.

Ramsay, Paul. "Elements of a Biblical Theory of Law." *Journal of Religion,* Volumes 29–30, October 1949.

Sadeler, William. "Kant on International Relations." *Journal of Philosophy,* December 9, 1954.

Schweitzer, Albert. "The Evolution of Ethics." *The Atlantic Monthly,* Volume 202, No. 5, November 1950.

Sekulow, Jay. *Law and Justice,* May–June 1993.

———. *Casenotes,* February 1994.

Slaatte, Howard A. "Social Ethics." *The New Christian Advocate,* September 1958.

Stringfellow, William. "The Christian Lawyer as a Churchman." *The Christian Scholar,* Volume IX, No. 3, September 1957.

———. Review of *The Moral Decision,* by Edmund Cahn. *The Christian Scholar,* Volume X, No. 3, September 1957.

———. Review of *Religion, Morality and the Law,* edited by Arthur L. Harding. *The Christian Scholar,* Volume XI, No. 3, 1957.

Stumpf, Samuel Enoch. "Theology and Jurisprudence." *The Christian Scholar,* Volume XI, No. 3, September 1957.

INDEX

T

U

W

Z